PRAI

Been There Taught That

"I've always loved Gregg's writing. It's incredibly honest, heartfelt, and brave. There's no shortage of humor – often at his own expense. And there's a genuine understanding that the lessons you're learning from his piece are not preachy. They are lessons he lived, for better or worse. So, it hits home. It moves you. It changes you for the better. Those are also some of the characteristics of a great teacher. "Been There / Taught That" is a compelling memoir of such a teacher."

Melanie Khramer | Songwriter/Musician | Sirsy.com

"Keeping it real is what comes to mind when reading Weinlein's writing. He hits you in the face with cold hard truths and then calms you down with gentle reasoning. He is truly a visionary."

Joan Valentina | NYC actress | Director and playwright

"For at-risk students like myself, a teacher like Gregg Weinlein was a game changer. His honest and sensitive approach made an education not only accessible but, for the first time, truly relevant to our lives."

Sean Burton | Former Student

This memoir is dedicated to my children
BECKETT, BRYEL, JESSE, AND CHRISTINE

A child is father to the man;
And I could wish my days to be
Bound each to each by natural piety
-Willian Wordsworth

* * *

And to all my students during my thirty five years teaching

* * *

Also to Jason and Joanna
along with their staff at the Crisp Cannoli
Thank you for the time, place,
and too many coffees that made this book possible

* * *

And finally, to my editor, Jacqueline Hanzl.
Thank you for keeping me balanced and upright throughout
the long challenging journey to write this memoir.

Contents

CHAPTER ONE

E2 - Albany Hospital Psychiatric Ward

I've been walking through the middle of nowhere
Trying to get to heaven before they close the door

Boom! I was certain I heard the muffled sound of a gunshot from the room across from mine. But did I? The horrific sound shattered the silence of the early morning. Was the sound really that of a gunshot?

I was still drugged up and given more pills at the hospital. Zombie-like. Did I really hear a gunshot? Or was the frightening sound just a screeching conclusion to another nightmare during my residency in the psychiatric ward of Albany Hospital? I wasn't sure.

The next morning, all patients were escorted to an emergency counseling session. We were informed of a patient suicide. No nightmare. Just a sick reality. A visitor managed to bring a gun to the patient.

The medical staff appeared shocked. Sincerely concerned. A few staff members were crying. The patients seemed disinterested. Detached.

I was sixteen years old.

A few days earlier my parents rushed me to the Albany Medical Center Emergency Room. I had punched my hand through the living room window at home. I was stoned and dazed by the combination of cheap alcohol, grass, and whatever drugs were floating around that evening at Ridgefield Park. I was out of control, completely lost my way, and didn't care. I just didn't care. I remember shouting that I didn't care if I died. When I started spitting up blood, my father swung me over his shoulder and carried me to the station wagon.

The skin on my hand was stitched back together. My parents and I were taken to another wing in the hospital.

A nurse and a doctor talked at length to my mother and father. I heard only fragments of their conversation. I faded in and out of consciousness; too *out of it* to care about their discussion. I started falling asleep in a chair.

An attendant in medical scrubs shook my shoulders vigorously. I had passed out and struggled to lift my head.

"Just sign down here." He handed me a clipboard and a pen.

"What's this?" I mumbled.

"Just sign it. Put your name here. Your parents signed already. Here." He lifted my arm and placed my hand on the clipboard where I was told to sign. I couldn't maintain control of the pen in my hand. He guided my hand to the bottom of the page. "Just initial here. That'll be easier."

Easier seemed good to me. Without knowing what I signed, the document now bore my scribbled initials. And I was too spaced out to care about what I signed.

I just wanted to sleep. To crash in peace.

Suddenly two security guards arrived. They were joined by several members of the hospital staff. I turned and looked at my parents.

"Gregg," stated the biggest security guard, "we're going to take you to your room."

"What are you talking about?" I clutched the arms of the chair with all my remaining strength. "I ain't going to no room here!"

The two security guards unwrapped my fingers and lifted me from the chair. I resisted, but to no avail.

"Don't make this difficult," the shorter guard with a Charles Bronson mustache stated. They dragged me towards a large, gray, steel door. My mother was crying. From a pocket of his pants, the taller guard pulled out a long chain with an assortment of keys to unlock the door.

I knew I didn't want any part of this madness. I was weak but fought viciously. Kicking. Punching. Screaming. When I kicked one of the guards in the balls and knocked him down, a doctor pulled out a needle from his white medical coat and stabbed my arm.

I became animalistic. I fought for my survival. But I lost this battle in minutes. More security guards came upon the scene and I was pinned to the floor. All I could move was my head. All I could hear was my screaming. "Get your fucking hands off of me!"

The injection soon rendered me motionless.

I was carried into a room and set onto a padded floor. The walls were also cushioned with blue pads.

A nurse knelt on the floor beside me and spoke. But between the chatter from the hospital staff, and my weakened screams for help, I was unable to hear what she was saying to me.

Soon everyone left. The door closed loudly. The staff exited.

I was alone. The room was dark. Completely dark. I was uncertain of my whereabouts. And was scared. Exhausted. Sick. I managed to crawl to the door. But I was locked inside. My head dropped onto the padded floor. Comatose.

When I awoke, I was in a bed in a hospital room. I tried to sit up but I was dead weight. I had lost all sense of time and place.

A food service staff member carried a tray of breakfast food with coffee to my bedside. I wasn't hungry.

"Where am I?"

"E2, son. The luxury suite of Albany Hospital." He started to laugh. Funny? I wasn't feeling the humor. Sliding down into the bed, I covered my face with blankets and slept again.

I was awake when a young nurse walked into the room with water and a small paper cup containing two pills.

"Good afternoon, Gregg. I'm your nurse for today."

"Hi. What time is it?" I was rubbing my still tired eyes. "How long did I sleep?"

"Three-thirty. You had a good rest. Now I need you to take your medication." A gentle face stood over me. That was my first impression when I looked at the nurse. A face that was not attached to a person I fought with while resisting being taken to the padded room. Just a face. A gentle face projecting a calming presence.

"What are these?" I lifted the cup. "What am I taking?" (Eventually I was informed that I was prescribed Thorazine, a very strong antipsychotic drug. Was I that fucked up?) "This is kind of funny. I took too many pills to get into the hospital...and now I get more pills inside. What are they for?"

"The pills will help you stay calm. Keep you at ease. Keep you balanced. Your admission was very combative and difficult. I was in the room they took you to last night. You were a wild young man. Out of control." The nurse added smiling, "And I want to be the nurse for a more peaceful Gregg. And the hospital wants you to be relaxed while you are here."

But I was agitated. "What do you mean '*while you are here*'? I want out of this place. No hard feelings. But I want out. Now!"

"Take your medication, Gregg. Take the edge off. The doctors will be in soon to explain everything."

CHAPTER TWO

My Hospital Residency

Above all, don't lie to yourself.

— Dostoyevsky —

I met with a group of doctors and nurses in a conference room. I was reluctant to share information. I felt like I had been duped. The whole process of being admitted to the hospital was a sham.

I was in no mood for a conversation. Nor was I about to trust anyone in the room. I answered only a few questions. Reluctantly and with an attitude. I was cautious and felt like I needed to protect myself. When a question was asked that I didn't want to answer, I sat in silence. The questions I did answer centered around basic information. Only what I was willing to share with the doctors and nurses.

"Tell us about school," a nurse threw out the first softball question I was willing to answer.

"I don't go to school. Didn't want to go. I dropped out in the first quarter." My responses were unrevealing and guarded.

A doctor, wearing a dress shirt and tie under his doctor coat, was up next, "What was going on in your life that made dropping out a viable option for you?" He wore wire-rimmed glasses. "Difficulties with your grades? Other students? Things going on at home?"

Silence.

Another nurse, much older than the one I met earlier in my hospital room, took her turn, "What year were you in at school when you dropped out?"

"Senior."

"Your last year of high school?" The nurse asked with a subtle hint of condemnation.

"You figured that out by yourself?" I was being a punk. Anger and snarkiness took over my personality. "I said I was a senior. That *is* the last year of high school." I hadn't recovered from my interaction with the staff the night before. Fuck all of them. "Do I get to ask a question?"

The doctor opened his arms and smiled as if to suggest he would welcome my question. Like sheep, the others on the medical team smiled along with the doctor. "What am I doing here? I was high last night. Messed up. That's all. Big deal. So why am I here?" I noticed a security guard standing at the door. Strange faces in complete control stared over me.

A staff member wearing blue scrubs lifted his head from notes on a legal tablet, "You are here because your parents brought you to the hospital. You put your hand through a window. You were violent and stated you were willing to harm yourself. Your parents did the right thing." He stated the details sounding very much like he was reading from a police report. "You were vomiting blood. You were drugged up and drunk." Mr. Scrubs continued, "You were fading in and out of consciousness. You had overdosed, Gregg. Do you remember what you took? And what did you drink last night?"

I remembered sharing a pint of blackberry brandy with Beth. And I drank from whatever bottle was passed around. And I remember Bucky had a pocketful of speed. Obederim. I helped myself to some of those. And there were joints being passed around and Sharon shared her hash pipe. And Lemily was running around the park, completely out of it, offering hits of acid. But if I took LSD last night I was already too far gone to remember. I responded with silence to Mr. Scrubs' question.

"We are all here to help you, Gregg," the doctor with the John Lennon specs suggested. "And you can help us...help you...if you can tell us what led to your self-destructive behavior last evening."

"I had a few beers." Like I said...I wasn't about to trust these people.

"And what else?" asked Mr. Scrubs. "We want to help you with your problem. All of us."

"Yeah...well, if you're helping me *get outta here...then you're helping me.*" My voice rose incredulously. "And then I won't even have a problem!"

"Eventually." Doctor Clipboard stated with authority. "When you are better and you receive the proper medical clearance from our team here...and after your seven day commitment period."

"What the hell does that mean?" I pounded the long wooden table and slouched down in my chair. "I want to leave now!"

"Gregg, your parents seemed in a hopeless position when they brought you here," the older nurse stated. "They were extremely worried. They signed a hospitalization document for the evaluation period. And then..." She looked through an assortment of papers and set one sheet on the table, "and then you signed this document with your initials. You will be here for seven days for evaluation and treatment."

"Noooooooo!" I screamed. "That's not fair! I was too fucked up to know what I was signing!" I bull rushed the security guard at the door. "This is bullshit! You can't do this. I didn't even know what I was signing. I need to get out. Now!"

I lunged toward the locked door knob. The security guard grabbed me and wrapped his large arms around mine. I was only able to kick relentlessly. My upper body was paralyzed by the guard's strength. I screamed. Repeatedly raging: "You can't keep me here! You can't keep me here!"

Another security guard entered and I was physically taken back to my seat. The two guards stood on each side of me.

Another nurse spoke. This one wore dark glasses and had tight wavy black hair that reminded me of the girls in the Elvis Presley movies. "Gregg, you will be seeing us every day you are here. You don't realize it now but we are here to help you. And we will help you. You are committed here for seven days. I want you to do your best, take advantage of our medical services, and make your stay a positive experience." Defeated, I dropped my head onto the table.

I didn't feel like I was admitted to the E2 Psychiatric Ward at Albany Hospital for seven days. I felt like I was sentenced. I didn't want to be here. I wanted to be free. And accepted. I wanted to feel like a sixteen year old again.

During my week at the hospital, nothing matched the fear and confusion I felt hearing the gun go off in the early morning hours during my first night in my room. Not that my hospital stay was without memorable events and interactions. But compared to the gunshot suicide in the room near me, my remaining days in E2 seemed uneventful.

For a couple of days I resisted introductions and conversations. I stayed focused on trying every angle I could think of to get discharged. I pleaded with the doctors during my evaluation sessions: "I really don't belong in this hospital. You know I'm not like the others here."

I threatened lawsuits, "How can you keep me here? I was so wasted. I didn't even know what I was signing. I was wrecked and too spaced out on drugs to know what I was signing. That has to be illegal." (I know… there are jailhouse lawyers so why not be a psych ward lawyer?)

I called Dr. Anolik, my psychiatrist I was seeing for months before my hospitalization and begged him to get me discharged.

And I begged my parents to get me out.

My efforts were emotional and exhausting. And to no avail. Despair was an uninvited spirit into my life. But I was streetwise. I knew seven days could be a countdown. And I knew I had to lessen the weight from the chains of despair.

I was stuck within the confines of a special section of Albany Hospital reserved for the deranged and addicted. And I was labeled one of them. The youngest. If I entered the hospital depressed, confused, and wasted, my existence here so far only led to heavy doses of hopelessness.

I felt like I was shoved into another arena where I had to prove myself. I prayed for the strength to cope. To endure. To survive. To get out. I wondered if my friends even knew of my hospitalization. And if so, I wondered what they thought of me now. A song by the Doors, *When The Music's Over,* continuously played in my head. When I felt defeated, I whispered the lyrics, *"Cancel my subscription to the resurrection."*

I was uncertain if I would rise again. What if I was unable to rebound? To be part of anything. To face anyone. To accept all the mistakes I made. And to be accepted by all the people I hurt by my actions. I foresaw a pending avalanche of despair. When I entered the hospital I was sick, depressed, and dangerous to myself. I was without purpose. And without direction.

I soon began to trust the nurse who delivered my medications to me. A first step. She was younger than the other staff members. She said she was still taking college courses and getting through the field experiences she needed for her nursing license.

Her *field experience* with me included: pill deliveries, checking my numbers, asking how I was feeling, and reminding me each morning of my appointments.

And she always stayed on after completing her nursing duties with me. She spent time with me to talk. Her name was Marie.

When I reflect on my days in E2, I think Nurse Marie was the reason I survived. She was sensitive and understanding - a big sister. I revealed more to Marie than I did with others on the medical team. And much more than the scraps of my life I offered during group counseling sessions.

Each morning after consuming my medication, taking my temperature, and checking my blood pressure, Nurse Marie would slide the visitor chair closer to my bed to rap with me.

I don't remember her last name. I have boxes of writings from my teenage years stored away. I haven't opened them since my stay in E2. They are stored in a file cabinet in the garage. I'm afraid of those writings. Afraid of the darkness of my teenage years that filled those pages. To this day, I refuse to open those boxes. I remain afraid the Genie of Pain and Guilt would erupt from those poems, and stories, and journals. Some day. *Maybe.* But I am sure, on one of those pages, I would have scribbled Marie's last name.

CHAPTER THREE

My Student Nurse

Will You be there each time I need you
And will you come each time I call to you

— Julie Vega —

"Did you grow up in Albany, Gregg?" For the first few visits my conversations with Marie were very protective and perfunctory. I always detoured from any hint of an inquisition that I felt was unnecessarily personal. But talking with Marie soon became a welcomed exchange of thoughts.

"My whole life. I always lived in Albany. Downtown. Near the Capitol when I was just a kid. That was a long time ago. I lived near where they are building the South Mall. And then we moved to upper Madison Avenue across the street from St. Rose College. What about you? Are you from Albany?"

"No." Marie sipped her coffee. "Downstate. From Long Island." Nurse Marie had long brown hair that she kept in a ponytail. Her eyes were the same color. "I came up here for college…for my nursing degree."

Despite my reluctance to converse openly, talking in a friendly manner with someone was life affirming and uplifting, even though our talks were mostly my responses to Nurse Marie's many questions. Each day my nurse departed my hospital room with another chapter of my mini-autobiography.

She knew my Mom and Dad had eight children. And that I was the fourth oldest. She knew my mother stayed home to raise the children. And that my father was a milkman who also worked an assortment of cleaning jobs on the side to help *keep the family above water.*

Marie knew all the Weinleins went to the neighborhood Catholic school. She asked, "How did your parents afford to send eight kids to a private school?"

"My father was the maintenance worker in the evening for the Vincentian Elementary School." I answered. "There was no cost... tuition was a job benefit." Years later, whenever I recalled our conversations, I realized the biographical information flowed in only one direction. I shared so much of my life story with Marie, but I got to know very little about her.

"And what about school, Gregg? Did you like school?" Her tone was always welcoming and sincere.

"I think I did. Depends." I knew the school topic would eventually hit a roadblock. I reminisced out loud. "I was a happy kid. Never really thought about school being something I liked, or didn't like. I just went to school. Every day. The school is practically in our backyard. I remember our mornings being a mad rush of routines to get out of the house. Every day was chaotic - all of us trying to get ready at the same time. That's what I remember about school the most - the craziness of getting ready to go. Jesus..." I reveled in the childhood memories.

"And your Mom had to manage all of you each morning?"

"Yeah. My father was already on the milk route. We all argued before school - who got to use the bathroom first, and getting in each others' way trying to get ready." And then I thought a thought I never thought before. "My poor mother."

Marie commented, "I'd say she's a special woman."

"Yeah. It's sad...you know? Thinking about my mother. I mean we all take her for granted. We live in a large building that is part of the school. It's called the Technical Building. The VI kindergarten classes are outside my bedroom door in the front of the building and we lived in the back. The house is so big."

Marie continued, "And were you an OK student?"

"I guess. I mean my grades were good, nothing special...but average. But then things started falling apart in high school when I was a junior."

"Something happened to you?"

The roadblock dropped before me. I heard the squeal of brakes to my life story. *Do Not Enter.* A shell of secrecy descended upon me. I realized I was drifting into a place I did not want to go. The willingness to converse with my nurse ceased. Sinking into the quicksand of the past year, I quickly assessed our talks as too inquisitive.

The silence in the room urged Marie to ask again, "So are you going to tell me what happened? What happened in your junior year? Is it connected to why you are here?" I locked up. Froze. I could feel the hurt that masked my face. I turned away from my nurse and glared at the side wall. "Maybe another time…OK, Gregg?" She sensed the door to my past year had closed. "I don't mean to pry." She stood from her chair. "Besides, I need to check in on some other patients. Do you want anything downstairs when I go down on my break?"

I turned from the wall and looked at Marie. I shook my head no. She smiled.

I tensed up. I crashed into the roadblock and didn't know where to go. My body froze. I watched Marie leave my room and vigorously clenched my fists.

I missed my bedroom stereo and my record collection. If I were home, I would have taken the *Aftermath* album by the Stones from a stack of records in a milk crate. The phonograph needle would have been placed on my favorite track so I could sing along with Mick: "I see a red door and I want it painted black".

CHAPTER FOUR

Finding My Voice With LeRoy

We gotta get out of this place
If it's the last thing we ever do

— Eric Burdon —

Two attendants made a loud entrance into my room and woke me up. I was taken to a large conference room for an emergency meeting with the staff and the other patients. The atmosphere was somber. For the first time, I realized the cold and salient stench of the E2 wing of the hospital. There was no warmth, no camaraderie, and only a seemingly feigned sensitivity in this section of the hospital.

The patients scattered onto gray metal chairs. A few were incapable of sitting and bounced about in constant manic motion. Some other residents preferred the floor and curled up against the wall. And others stood like scarecrows unstable in a heavy wind storm.

LeRoy, a smack junkie whose room was adjacent to mine, sat next to me. The hospital staff sat in the front at a long conference table. For this meeting we were joined by two uniformed Albany cops, and between them was a suited middle-aged man who introduced himself as Detective *Somebody.* A priest was also on the panel for our emergency gathering. Father *Somebody.*

But I was in no mood for authority figures. And I wasn't in the mood for God. I was sixteen years old. Did I believe in God? I wasn't even sure if I believed in myself.

We were introduced to the E2 medical staff. A few I already knew. But no one I connected with except Nurse Marie. Scary, but I think I felt simpatico with my fellow patients: disinterested, tired, and just wanting to leave. We listened like detached space cadets. Some patients were more permanently out of their minds than others. Some were unjustly born that way. Some residents were victims of life's cruelties. And some were damaged goods by the consequences of their own bad decisions. I knew which label was mine.

Dr. Clipboard began the meeting. "We had a tragedy on our wing of the hospital. Last night, a gun was smuggled into a patient's room." He paused as if to regroup. "The patient committed suicide."

My fellow patients in the room didn't seem to care.

Dr. Clipboard continued with a tone of sympathy and proper organizational dynamics, "Please…if you saw anything related to the gun being brought into the room, or if you heard or knew anything, or if you know a patient is contemplating suicide, let a staff member know. We want you to get better during your stay here. To take care of yourself; not harm yourself. If you know another resident is contemplating suicide, please inform us. There will be a full investigation for the next few days so there will be others walking around our floor. Professionals you have never seen before."

I glanced at the patients in the conference room. I wondered if any of the residents knew what the word *contemplating* meant. Doubt it. But I was certain they were not interested in learning the definition.

Father *What's His Name* nodded in saintly agreement.

Detective *I Forgot His Name* did a visual scan of every patient in the room. His glare was meant to instill fear. Authoritarianism at its finest.

Patient Gregg smiled at LeRoy and thought: here I am, sixteen years old, sitting in a psych ward next to a junkie decades older, and listening to a report about a guy who blew his brains out. And suddenly a flashback: just months ago I was playing in a Connie Mack baseball league on a team my father coached.

Erratic and dangerous was the treacherous path of my life.

An older nurse moved to the center of the panel to speak. "What happened last night was so troubling. The incident will cause a variety of intense feelings in many of you. Now would be a good time to share our feelings about last evening's tragedy." "Here we go again. Same old bullshit," mumbled LeRoy.

"Talk with us about how you are internalizing the tragedy." The perfectly starched uniformed nurse continued, "What are your thoughts? How are you dealing with the suicide? Anyone?"

Last night the gunshot was loud, terrifying, and deadly. This morning the silence in the conference room was numbing.

After two full days on E2, I still didn't know the names of most staff members or patients. But I knew LeRoy. He leaned towards me and whispered, "This is fucking beat, man. Crazy shit all of us having to be here."

LeRoy was a quiet, nervous man with a massive Afro. I guessed he was in his forties. He told me he drummed for a soul band, except at gigs when he was too junked up to play. Whenever I visited his room, we listened to his record albums. A girlfriend had brought a small record player to him. We listened to James Brown, Aretha, the Temptations, and the Ronettes. He had a serious crush on Ronnie Spector. Some nights I could hear LeRoy drumming on his meal table and singing, "Walking in the rain" or, "Be my baby."

Painfully, the silence lingered in the conference room. No one spoke. Minutes seemed like hours.

Dr. Clipboard asked, "Does anyone want to express their feelings? We would like to know how you are dealing with the loss of one of our community members." LeRoy nudged me, "Boy, you got to say something, these fucking crazies won't say a fucking word. And those bastards won't let us leave until they get what they want. We could be here forever! Speak your mind, kid. Say something. Tell them what you feel."

I surveyed the room. LeRoy was right. The *crazies* wouldn't speak. The glare in their eyes was intergalactic. Some of the patients probably didn't know they were in a conference room at a meeting.

"But I'm not *feeling* anything, LeRoy. I don't know what to say. Shit happens." "No one's feeling shit, boy. Just pretend you are. They'll buy your bullshit."

The nurse continued, "What we all experienced last evening was such an inconceivable and tragic loss. Just open up and freely express your feelings. Let it go. Tell us how you feel. We need to know so we can be here for each other."

"See what I mean, boy?", LeRoy whispered. "They don't quit. Help us out, kid. We gonna be here forever if you don't. They won't end this damn meeting until someone dishes out some bullshit. Say anything. You make sense when you talk. You're a smart one. Maybe the only one with a brain left on this floor. Speak up, kid, so these scrubs will let us go."

"OK", I responded hesitantly and without confidence. LeRoy nodded his appreciation. I lifted my head towards the front of the room, raised my hand as if I was still in school, and spoke, "Like...I mean..." I was nervous about being nervous.

"Could you stand?" Dr. Clipboard requested. "So everyone can hear you." "Yeah...," I stood reluctantly, "Like I don't think that it is any of my business. I'm dealing with my own crap. It was his life. His reasons." There was a hint of *I don't give a shit* arrogance in my voice. My confidence was enhanced knowing LeRoy sat beside me in welcomed approval.

"Are you troubled by the incident?" Dr. Clipboard asked. "This is a lot to take in - especially for someone your age. How old are you, Gregg?"

Wow. Someone besides Nurse Marie knew my name. "Sixteen."

"A teenager still. For certain what happened during the night will affect how you feel about your stay here." The doctor jotted something onto the paper of his clipboard. "And probably affect you for the rest of your life."

I think I smirked glancing down at LeRoy who whispered, "Keep rapping, kid...only way we get out of here."

I continued. "To be honest, I'm not troubled at all. It was his choice. Things must have been so shitty for him here that he didn't want to be part of it anymore. And you know what?" I hesitated. I was uncertain if I wanted to say what I wanted to say. But I did. "You know this place can make you feel that way. You said we are a 'community.'" I almost laughed. "I mean we all heard about what happened last night before this meeting. And there were times this morning... in my room...that I thought what happened last night wouldn't be a bad option." Another notation was written onto Dr. Clipboard's paper. "This is like the most unfriendly place ever. I mean I only know a few of you by name. And except for the nurse named Marie, you are the first person to call me by my name. Yeah. You and Nurse Marie. The only two who have called me by my name. And the only other person on E2 I've had a *real* conversation with is LeRoy. And I'm just 'boy' or 'kid' to him." I looked down at LeRoy who was smiling now at the thought of a pending exit from the meeting.

I nodded to my *community* support group co-residents. That was a meaningless gesture. But that didn't matter. LeRoy was there and I was determined to follow advice: speak up so this meeting would end. "You say you want us to get better, but this place is a rat trap of coldness and isolation. I'm just counting each day until I get out of here. And if I do make it out...I'm sure that suicide option will be off the table for me." I looked around again at my colleagues. "And I'm sure I'm not the only one who feels that way."

Maybe. Scanning the faces of the other residents, I thought to myself, there are some *real* crazies here...really fucking crazy. And I didn't belong here. I didn't need any more motivation to get through my time in E2 than that realization. I continued the exchange of bullshit with the hospital staff for a few more minutes. I guess the articulation of my feelings sufficed. The meeting concluded. LeRoy elbowed me and said, "Right on, kid." As I sat back in my chair, LeRoy gestured with his hand out, "Slap me some skin."

Doctor Clipboard made his final comment, "The police investigation is ongoing. And I want you to know the staff on E2 will continue to check in on your feelings and how you are internalizing the suicide. We will continue to be here for you."

That "be here for you" statement was nauseating.

LeRoy and I walked out of the conference room side by side. The detective glared at me in his best effort to intimidate. I sensed he thought I was antagonistic; a troublemaker; a wiseass.

"So help me God, kid...I'm gonna do whatever it takes - keep myself clean and stay away from the needles. No more skag. I don't ever want to come back again."

"I'm with you on that, LeRoy."

"Listen, kid - I ain't got a clue why you's here -but whatever the fuck is why- don't do it again. I'm telling you the deal, boy. If I ever see you in this place again, I'm gonna kick your ass." And then LeRoy began singing, *It's my life and I'll do what I want.* "You know that song, kid? The Animals. White peoples' band. But with a white blues singer with a lotta soul."

I looked up at LeRoy. I knew the band and was a fan. I responded by singing another lyric to an Eric Burdon song back at him, "We gotta get out of this place / If it's the last thing we ever do."

"You got that right." LeRoy smiled. "Ain't no joking there, Gregg."

The third person to call me by my name.

CHAPTER FIVE

Still Connected

Connection, I just can't make it, connection
But all I want to do is to get back to you

— Keith Richards —

I spoke with my parents every day on a payphone at the end of the hall. My first two days in the hospital, I told my mother and father I didn't want them to visit. I was ashamed of myself and embarrassed. And probably still blaming them for my residency on E2. But I soon slid into a pit of loneliness. And I also realized my roadblock to their visits was hurtful. Besides, after a few days I accepted that I was the one who fucked up. I was quickly sinking into an abyss of emptiness.

At the group meeting I was truthful when I said I was untroubled by the suicide in the room next to mine. Numb to feelings about that incident. What I did feel was the crushing blows of shame for being in the psychiatric ward. I wanted out. Not just from the hospital, but also from the debris of my life.

During the evening of Day Three at E2, shortly after dinner, I heard a commotion of voices in the hallway. The loud authoritarian voice of Nurse Meanie rose above the raucous, "I said you could visit but *only* three at a time. And no rowdiness. And quiet voices. Be respectful to the other patients with the noise level in his room."

My door opened and three of my best friends from Madison Avenue stormed in: Lemily, Beth, and Sharon. I didn't think they knew I was in E2.

"What the fuck you doing here, Gregg?" Lemily demanded without waiting for an answer. "We were supposed to catch Johnny's band at St. Andrews' on Saturday. No one knew where you were. We're all asking each other, 'Where the fuck is Gregg?' We knew something was wrong when you didn't show up to hear St. James' Infirmary."

"Yeah. Well..." I sheepishly stumbled for words. "I guess I took a detour."

"Wiseass," Beth noted, sitting at the end of the bed. "I went to your house every day and hounded your mother. She wouldn't say a thing. That's not like your mom not to talk to us. I knew some serious crap was going down. It was a bummer to see her like that."

I was more nervous and embarrassed than welcoming. "I'm sure she didn't want to talk about where I was."

Beth slid herself forward along the bed and grasped my hand. She was a few years younger than the others but she caught up to our world quickly. Probably too quickly. "Your mother looked sad. And she was so quiet. I didn't like seeing her like that. She didn't look like the mom we all know, Gregg. She was always so friendly and would spend time talking to any of us. She finally told me what went down this afternoon. We hustled over here so quickly. I was sworn to secrecy by your mother." Beth nodded towards my friends in the room. "But I guess I didn't do a good job with that."

Like a member of some clandestine military unit, Bucky snuck into the room pulling out a bottle of Ripple wine from his fatigue jacket. My fourth visitor, Bucky never was one to abide by rules. "What's this fucking gig, man?" He twisted the cap off his bottle and took a sip. "Bad trip?" Bucky always appeared permanently intoxicated even before he got drunk. "You drop some bad acid?" He walked over to the window and sat on the ledge. "Too much speed?" His sips of Ripple were rhythmic. "How do we get you the fuck out of here? This is some bad shit, dude. You just vanished. Ain't none of us had a fucking clue."

"Maybe Gregg doesn't want to talk about it," Sharon suggested.

The girls who hung with us were our teenage street social workers who knew when to put us into protective custody. Always trying to keep the guys in check. They weren't girlfriends. Nor were we boyfriends. But watch out if anyone messed with our girls. A calvary of adopted big brothers would be kicking some ass. Beth's ex-boyfriend from another neighborhood found that out quickly. We jumped him after we learned that he slapped Beth around.

"Doesn't matter what he did. It's Gregg's bag of shit." Lemily surmised, reaching into his jacket pocket and pulling out a pint bottle of blackberry brandy. "I got this for you to keep you company here. Pretend this is like the priests' wine we stole when we were altar boys. A sacred bottle with healing powers." Lemily presented his gift to me. "Everytime you take a swig, say to yourself, *the Lord be with me,* and you'll get OK and get your ass out of here real quick."

"Thanks, Lem. You're crazy," I noted. "You're the one who should be in this place instead of me." My comfort level with my friends was returning to normal. "Yeah. Can you imagine? If we were ever here together?" Lemily thought and surmised. "We'd take over the fuckin' place in no time. *Up against the walls, motherfuckers.*" Lemily quoted from his favorite MC5 song. "Just let them try to keep me here. They got you, Gregg. But they ain't getting me."

We laughed loudly. All of us. Too loudly. An alarm for raucous behavior must have sounded. Nurse Meanie, who cautioned my friends in the hallway, stormed into the room. She saw Bucky drinking from his wine bottle. "Out! Get out now! You can't bring alcohol in here!" Her face reddened with rage. I hid my brandy under the pillow. "Leave now!" The nurse ordered. "Or I will call security. I warned you! Three in a room and no disruptive behavior. You can't follow simple rules?" She reached for Bucky's bottle.

"Whoooooa! Back off there, Lady." Bucky ordered. "Sorry, Nurse. If I'm leaving, my bottle's leaving with me." He put the Ripple back into his jacket pocket. Bucky was our jailhouse lawyer. "You can't throw them out." He slapped at his pocket that contained his bottle. "You can throw me out. It was my bottle and I'm the one drinking." His sudden transformation was dramatic. "You see…I got a problem." Bucky feigned sadness. "I think I'm in the wrong part of the hospital. Got a problem with the drink, you know? It's in my genes. My parents…you know…alcoholics. I mean, being a good nurse and everything, you understand, right? These guys didn't even know I had a bottle with me when I came in." Bucky's hand gestured to the crew in the room. "I'm the bad guy here. I'm the fourth visitor and I snuck in here violating your rules. I surrender. Guilty as charged."

"I still want all of you to leave the room…and the hospital. And I want you to leave this instant."

"I'm going. I'm going." Bucky reached over to shake my hand. He turned back to Nurse Meanie. "But fair is fair. They're innocent." He nodded to his three comrades in the room. "Dig? I'll leave now. But at least give them some extra time to visit. They just got here. I mean Beth and Sharon are Gregg's sisters." Bucky lied. "And the dude's Gregg's cousin." Bucky lied again. "Family. That wouldn't be right to throw them out because of me."

"Then you get out right now," the nurse pointed her finger at Bucky. "And I mean now. Immediately. His sisters and cousin can stay. But only for five minutes." Nurse Meanie marched Bucky towards the door. Before she exited, she turned to warn us, "And I'll be standing right at the door. Any more raucous, and all of you leave."

But Bucky had to have the last word. From the doorway he yelled back to me. "You get out of here, Gregg. I don't like the people who run this place."

CHAPTER SIX

Loneliness Talks

I'm a poor man's son,
From across the railroad tracks

— Stevie Wonder —

After my friends left, I went over to my neighbor's room. LeRoy said he could hear the commotion in my room. I told him my friends got kicked out. Laughing, he noted, "Be careful, boy. The hospital gonna see your friends as a symptom of your sickness. Give 'em more to evaluate. More time to lock you up here."

I had a few paperbacks and a notebook for my poems on a gray metal meal table. On LeRoy's table were a pair of Ludwig drumsticks and his record player. "My friend Lemily showed up with a present. A pint of blackberry brandy." I took the bottle out from the waistband of my jeans. "I stashed the bottle under my pillow when the nurse barged in."

LeRoy's eyes lit up. "You got to share the goods, kid. Don't leave me cold." He reached out for the bottle. "Nice your friends visited. No one been here for me. Ain't got no family around." He held the bottle closer to his face to read the label. "Most of my friends are junkies too, so they ain't coming here. And the guys in the band are disgusted with me. For sure they ain't visiting."

"I'll bring the brandy over to drink tonight after dinner if we can listen to your 'Uptight' album. I love that song. Kind of relate to it."

"Yeah…we can do the brandy and listen to Stevie. I'll put the album on the turntable and we can have our own little hospital party. Your friends know why you at E2?"

"Never got around to telling them. But they probably know."

"You ain't never told me either, kid. But I don't give a damn. I fucked up. You fucked up. And we's here. Friends don't need to know all your shit. They just need to trust you's friends. Listen, kid - any fool can do stupid shit to get their ass in this place. But you got to be cool to get yourself out."

LeRoy's advice became my ticket out of E2. My mantra for survival. Day Four. I had exhausted all attempts to reduce my seven day commitment at Albany Med.

My attitude now was not to do a damn thing wrong to extend my stay. Like LeRoy said, I *got to be cool.*

Back in my room, Nurse Marie stopped in to check on me. She gently lifted my bandaged hand and asked if I still felt pain. She did this with every visit. My connection with her grew stronger each day. Maybe too strong. I liked my nurse. I really liked her. And I trusted her. I felt the same sense of companionship with Marie that I feel with Beth, and Sharon, and the other girls from Madison Avenue. A connection of understanding and sensitivity. Still, I remained steadfast in my hesitancy to reveal personal details. But as my comfort level with Marie grew, I started to open up during our conversations.

"At the end of my junior year I failed American History." I informed my nurse. "Final average for the year, including the final exam, was sixty-four and a third. I'm not kidding. I begged for an extra credit assignment. Anything to get my grade changed to a sixty-five. Less than one crappy point. Nope. Not with Brother Leo dishing out grades."

"Wow," Marie exclaimed. "That's cruel. Was sixty-four and a third actually on your report card?"

"No. The jerk being the ass he is, he put sixty-four on my report card. My final average was rounded down. But if you add the four quarters, and the final, and divide by five, my grade was sixty-four and a third."

"Did you talk with the principal?" Marie inquired.

"My father did. He talked to Brother Leo and then went to the principal. I was sure something would happen that would get me through. Especially with the Bear. That was the nickname I gave my father and it stuck. We all called him The Bear. He knew every person in the school since he did the maintenance work. I was certain that I would get the grade rounded out to sixty-five and I'd pass and get the credit. Two thirds of a point."

"And?"

"Not with Brother Leo. He was such a hard-ass. He beat some students...and failed others. So that's how my junior year ended. Failing American History. I passed the class in summer school, but then I dropped out and didn't go back to school in the Fall."

"On your intake, the info noted you weren't going to school when you were checked in to E2. Did you drop out because of the American History class?"

"No. I mean...I mean I guess so - indirectly. But there was so much other shit going on in my life. I knew I couldn't handle being in school. So much crap going on in my life." Someone was about to trespass into the sanctuary of my guilt and despair. I retreated into my protective shell. "I don't want to talk about that now."

I could feel the intense emotional collision of sadness and anger that accompanied my flashbacks to summer and fall before I was admitted to E2. I glared into my coffee to silence myself.

Marie stood from her chair. She knew I had locked down. "Maybe another time, Gregg. If you want to talk, you know I'm here to listen. I better get to my other patients before someone complains."

CHAPTER SEVEN

Tapping Into the Secrets

Won't you come see me, Sweet Marie

— Bob Dylan —

I struggled on Day Five. The visits from Marie were an emotional oasis from the darkness and loneliness of my existence at E2. She made me feel like I was still able to connect with the world. As much as I depended on her visits and our conversations, I selfishly never thought about her school and work schedule; or her life outside the hospital. I took her presence for granted.

But today was Marie's day off from the hospital.

I stayed in my room. Lemily and Sharon visited me again. This time without a bottle. They hung with me longer than their first visit. No time limit to their visit since Nurse Meanie was not on duty. Sharon finally asked how I ended up at the hospital. But even with my best friends, I was evasive.

"Took some pills at the park." I minimized my explanation. "You know...like we all were doing. I didn't even know what they were. And I know I drank too much. I drank and popped whatever was being passed around." I tried to play off my overdose as an accident. But what I drank was no accident. And all the pills I took were without thought and recklessly swallowed.

"I didn't hear 'bout nothing new going down." Lemily offered. "Surprised you got so fucked up."

"I don't know...maybe it was the hits of acid I got from you." I deflected with a smile. "Whatever...everything together just fucked me up. When I got home from Ridgefield I was throwing up blood. Never had that happen before. Scared the hell out of my mother. I heard her yell to the Bear to get me to the hospital. Next thing I know is I signed some paper in the emergency room. I was still all messed up. Didn't even know what the hell I was signing. But the next day, I found out that whatever I signed committed me to this place for seven days."

"But what about your hand?" Sharon looked down at my bandages and continued with her inquisition. "We got kicked out so quickly the other night because of Bucky, we didn't even get to ask you what happened."

"That's a long story." Not really. Before I collapsed at home I exploded and angrily punched my hand through the living room window. But to Sharon I responded, "Another time."

"Dig." Sharon accepted. "But the good news is you only have two days left, right? When you get out of here, Gregg, you gotta take it down. You've been out of control. We all see it, man. If you don't care about yourself and keep getting wasted...I don't know, but I can tell you, your mom isn't handling all this shit well. And your father... Bear just seems angry and confused."

After Sharon and Lemily left, guilt and sadness blanketed me. I didn't care about hurting myself. But I didn't want to hurt anyone else - especially my parents. I walked the long corridor to the payphone and called my mother. "I'm sorry for this, Mom. I get out of here on Friday. Just two days left. When I get out, I promise I'm going to get my act together. I promise."

"We love you, Gregg." I could sense the pain in her voice. "And we miss you. We want you back home so much."

I apologized again. And promised again.

I was sullen and quiet during my appointment with my E2 psychiatrist. I still wasn't giving up anything about myself. Just being cool. I hung on to LeRoy's mantra. When I spoke I only talked about my discharge date and all the positive things I intended to do for myself to avoid ever returning to E2.

"Healthy intentions, Gregg," the Doctor acknowledged. "But the challenge is that reality seldom falls in line simply with life affirming intentions. I know this is a cliché, but our lives are like puzzles with multiple pieces. So many pieces in a lifetime." His words were emphasized by hand gestures and facial expressions. "We place a piece here...wrong choice. So then you try another...and maybe still another. Some pieces fall right into place. And that's great. But in life, we are often challenged to find the right piece." The Doctor had imaginary puzzle pieces in his hand and attempted to put a puzzle together on his glass top desk. "Some fit right away...and others don't. And you can get frustrated trying. Even sink into despair. And then you give up and that's when you lose. You understand, right?"

"I do. But I think I lost the game not even knowing what puzzle in my life I was trying to put together."

"Explain yourself to me, Gregg. What do you mean?" The doctor's puzzle demonstration ended. He leaned back in his oversized chair and he folded his hands.

"I don't know. I'm not sure. But I understand what you're telling me. I have to keep myself in check when the right piece isn't put into the right place."

"You see, Gregg, you don't want to set yourself up for another setback. So you can't just assume getting out of the hospital by itself is your ticket to putting your life back together. You're sixteen. You will make many more mistakes throughout your life. Bad choices. There will be setbacks and you will be confronted with numerous challenges. And that is when you have to tap into your resilience so you handle those setbacks."

"I get that. But at least getting out of here puts me on first base."

The psychiatrist smiled. I think he appreciated my baseball analogy. In my remaining group sessions I became more engaged. I felt sorry for so many of the patients on E2. Poor souls. I had a clue about my life and a desire to figure out a game plan for myself. Can witnessing the deficits of others be a motivator in life?

I became more positive and confident during the final days of my stay in E2. I became a team player and took on the unexpected role of an advocate. Despite being much younger, LeRoy told me other patients looked to me as a leader.

I remember one argument with the medical team I initiated during a group session. I protested that all our discussions were about how fucked up we were. And how we feel about being fucked up. I protested to the counselors and social workers, "Every damn session we come in here and you just want us to go off on how screwed up we are. We know that already. Most of us *do know where we are.* You get admitted to E2 if you're screwed up. But you insist that we keep rapping about how messed up we are and about how hopeless we are. How the hell are we supposed to look ahead if we only talk about how we screwed things up in the past to get us here?"

A nurse responded, "We are here to help you address those issues and help you work through your problems." I was so sick of her *here to help you* spin. She was the same nurse who threw Bucky out of my room. Nurse Meanie. I wasn't too friendly.

"Ain't gonna happen...not the way things go down here. This is my fifth day and I don't know any of you...and I know you really don't know me." I was agitated. I could have used a chug of Lemily's blackberry brandy right now. "And I don't trust any of you so I stay tight lipped and clam up."

LeRoy gently punched my leg. Smiling, he whispered, "Getting down, kid. Right on, brother. Talking some nitty-gritty now."

The next day the patients were beckoned to the large meeting room. On a long clothed table there was pizza, soda, and cookies for dessert. And *no* questions. A record player was set up and we listened to the Beatles. A new deck of playing cards was set on each table. I stood by the window. The sun was shining and there was a brilliant glare through the bars on the large pane. I smiled at the thought that I would be outside soon. A few more days.

LeRoy walked over to me with two slices of pizza on a paper plate. He smiled. "These fuckups never seemed so happy. I gotta tell you something, Gregg." He called me by my name. "Once you out, you best remember if I ever see you back in this joint, I'm gonna whup your white ass. You got the goods to do something with your life. Don't fuck that up."

After our social hour, Marie stopped into my room with my afternoon pills. Thorazine always made me sleepy and at times, even loopy. She also had two bags of M&M'S and two coffees from the cafeteria. "Here." She set the treats and coffee on the table. "This coffee is so much better and fresher than the hospital cafeteria coffee they bring to your room up here."

I stopped writing in my poetry notebook. I was so happy to see her. "I didn't know you had yesterday off. I don't know why, but I didn't even think of you having a schedule. And that there would be days you have off and wouldn't be here."

"I wish they felt like days off. Because when I'm not here, I'm working on school assignments and going to classes. I don't know which part of my life is easier - school or the hospital? Take your pills, Gregg. I'll be right back." Marie left the room and returned momentarily with another chair. "Getting tired of only seeing you in your hospital bed. We can each sit in a chair now. More comfortable for us, and you will look more like a patient getting out of here in a few days."

"Thanks, Marie." I stepped out of the bed with Marie assisting me with my bandaged hand.

"I heard you stole the show yesterday at your group session. One of the nurses described your speaking out as a 'breakthrough.' And she also said the doctors were impressed by your empathy."

I adjusted myself in the chair and faced Marie. "I guess nothing is kept quiet here. Wouldn't think that would be their opinion. I kind of told them off."

"Well, I think what they saw was a sense of compassion and awareness...and a feisty spirit willing to speak out for others."

"Yeah...whatever." I wasn't impressed that they were impressed. I only wanted my final days to go by quickly. "The pizza they got us was the worst I ever ate." Marie laughed. She poured cream into my coffee. "And one sugar, right?" She remembered. "The other day you froze up on me when we got to you dropping out of school. You said you passed the American History class in summer school. But then you didn't go back to school in September?"

I didn't know we would be continuing our conversation where we left off. But momentarily, I felt less protective and defensive. I was just glad Marie was back at the hospital and in my room. I lowered my guard. "No. I had enough of Brother Leo and that bull crap. I swore to myself I would never go back to VI." (He wasn't the main reason. But that was a good excuse.)

"Seems like a lot to quit on...just because of one bad teacher. I thought you said you did well at VI. Didn't you say you went to school there since kindergarten?"

"Yeah. A lotta years." I opened a bag of M&M'S.

"And all your siblings went to school there too?" I nodded. "And your father worked at the elementary school and your family lived in the back of the VI kindergarten building? That school sounds like a big part of your family's life."

"Yeah." I was smiling at Marie's succinct description of my existence. "That's where we lived. Behind the two kindergarten classrooms. My bedroom was right behind the upstairs kindergarten classroom." I ate a few more pieces of candy.

"Seems like a lot to throw away just because of Brother Leo. Seems crazy." I made eye contact with Marie and, for the first time, noticed the inviting assuring sparkle in Marie's expressive eyes. "You just decided not to go back to school in September, even though you earned the History credit in summer school?"

"No. I didn't drop out right away. I tried school. I transferred to Albany High School. And I hated it. The place was so big. So many kids at that school. I was used to the smaller scene after all the years at VI. And I was hassled every day by the principal at Albany. He pulled me aside every goddamn day and told me to get a haircut. Like I was the only one there with long hair. During the summer I let my hair grow and kept it really long. Like it is now." I watched Marie open the other bag of M&M'S and drop a few onto her napkin. "I felt like I was being picked on at Albany High because other kids there had hair longer than mine. I didn't last long there before I dropped out. The only good part about going to Albany High was my friend, Johnny. He's a singer in a band that plays a lot of weekend dances and college parties. Johnny would pick me up in his Mustang convertible and take me to school every day. His father was a big time lawyer. I felt so cool. Do you go to the frat parties at any of the colleges? Johnny's band is called St. James's Infirmary."

"I don't get to go out much. Don't do much of anything. I don't think I have a life besides school and my work here. I can't slip up and have to stay focused. I really want to get my nursing license this year." Marie ate some M&M'S. The moment of silence seemed like an eternity. "Help me get this straight, Gregg. I think I am missing something. You quit VI because of a teacher who failed you? Enrolled in Albany High, but you didn't like the large student population and the principal who hassled you about your hair? But when you were at Albany High, you got a ride to and from school each day by a friend who drove a Mustang? And then you just dropped out? And not too long after dropping out...you made your way here, to E2. Practically comatose. You were loaded up with so many drugs. What am I missing, Gregg? There has to be other reasons why you just gave up on everything."

"Yeah. But I don't look at it that simply. When you lay it down like you do, it does seem crazy - dropping out and everything." My momentary openness was quickly closing. "I was messed up too... drinking a lot and taking drugs every day. There was a lot of other crap that went down and I couldn't cope."

Marie placed one empty coffee cup into the other. She wiped the table clean with a napkin. "Gregg, we talk everyday. Sometimes more like friends than your nurse and my patient. But you only drop scraps of your life on me. You're very puzzling, Gregg. You keep everything surface level. Like you're not giving me all the puzzle pieces." My nurse stood from the chair and walked to the basket to deposit the napkins and coffee cups.

"I got the same *puzzle* rap earlier from my psych doctor, Marie. Do you have to leave now?" I felt nervous that she was departing.

"Don't have to." Marie answered standing by the basket near the doorway. One of my patients was discharged this morning so I have some more time. But..."

"Can you stay?"

"Yes...but I have to tell you, Gregg...I don't think you're leveling with me." She walked back towards my bed. "You know, when we have staff meetings, every person in the room knows you are holding back. We all know you didn't get here just because you drank too much and overdosed. We know that what you did that night was a drastic reaction hoping to escape from whatever it is you won't tell us. We know that drinking and drugs were your choice to self-medicate. We know you weren't just playing around consuming in a recreational manner. You were escaping from something. We all know that. So yeah, I can hang out longer with you today. But not for the head games. Not if you are only going to keep shutting me out from what really happened."

I dropped my head to my chest. I was embarrassed by the juxtaposition of my need for friendship and my need to keep secret what happened. I no longer wanted to make eye contact. Marie was too close. But I didn't want her to back off and leave. "Please stay. OK?"

Marie walked back towards my chair. Her hand brushed my shoulder gently. She sat back down into her chair. "Gregg, I really want to know why you dropped out of school and why you really ended up in E2."

CHAPTER EIGHT

Secrets No More

They never did like Mama's homemade dress
Papa's bank book wasn't big enough

— Bob Dylan —

Marie stayed and I talked. Maybe too much. I had held so much inside. Tried to pretend. Tried to evade. And I tried to present myself as being *soooo* together. The cool image I projected for myself on the outside was not the same volcanic reality within me. A charade. I had morphed into a self protective lie.

This is who you would have met at E2. This is what I ran with:

I was a teen with a steady girlfriend.

A baseball star selected to play in the Connie Mack League.

I was hip. Groovy. Wore a sportcoat with a Neru collar like the Beatles.

My friend Lemily and I *borrowed* the coats from the priests' wardrobe closet at St. Vincent de Paul Church. We were good altar boys. We didn't have the money to buy our own mod coats at Rosen's Department Store. So we *borrowed them.* I wore mine to the CBA school canteen, shows at St. Andrew's Church, and especially to the Sunday afternoon rock concerts at The Hideout to hear The Bougalieu. We knew Larry, the drummer in the band. Knew his whole family.

And I was so cool acting like Dylan. Both Bob Dylan and Dylan Thomas. A hard drinking teenage rebel who sang Dylan songs and quoted verses by the Welsh poet. And, to accent my image, my good friend Sheila made a black and white houndstooth scarf for me just like the one Bob Dylan wore on his *Blonde on Blonde* album cover.

And I was a reader of the Beat poets: Ferlinghetti, Ginsberg, Corso. And I was a cool, rebellious sixteen-year-old cigarette smoking poet. Too hip for my own good. But so damn *cool.*

And I was so talented at pretending I was someone I was not. I managed that facade throughout the summer and early fall. Just barely managed. And then...every fucking thing about me crashed.

And Marie, a nurse I have known for only a few days, was getting the first peek into the shattered glass of the barred window of my teenage abyss. She turned on the transistor radio my parents brought to me during a visit. "Some background noise, OK?" The Association's hit, "Cherish" was on the air. I was never a fan. Sentimental pop. But those top ten bands certainly got airplay. "You like this song, Gregg?"

"Not really." I responded politely, uncertain if this was Marie's type of music. "What music do you like?"

"I like a lot of the folk artists like Judy Collins and Joan Baez. What are you into?"

I didn't need to think much about my answer. "Stones, the Beatles. And I like the Animals. But I listen to Bob Dylan more than anyone else."

Marie leaned towards me with a gaze of sincerity in her brown eyes. Music was no longer going to be our topic of conversation. "I really want to know, Gregg." She held my hand. "Tell me what really happened. How did you end up here? I think school is just your go-to answer to avoid the real story. What's the real reason you dropped out and ended up in E2?"

"I don't know." I nervously adjusted myself in the chair. "Like it messes me up to talk about it. Even think about it. It hurts. I feel alone and stranded whenever I think about it. I know I screwed up.

Only my mother knows. I told her. But I'm sure she told my father. I don't think anyone else in my family knew at the time. I never said a thing to any of my friends. But I get the feeling everyone knows now. The end of my junior year at VI - like it was so hard. And I was scared. And I...I don't know...I guess..."

"You're rambling, Gregg." I could feel Marie's thumb gently rubbing my hand. "Just let it go and tell me. I'm not one to judge, Gregg. Promise."

And so I did. Reluctant. Maybe afraid. But I surrendered. Opened the wounds for the first time since I told my mother. I struggled to unveil *the secret* I hoped no one would know. How would I frame what really happened? And how would I articulate the hopelessness I felt? And I worried what Marie would think of me. I reluctantly began, "A group of VI kids were standing on Yates Street outside of school. We hung there every day at lunchtime to smoke cigarettes and just rap about anything...and everything. Parties in the park. Knapp's Tavern. Girlfriends."

Marie asked, "And?" Her eyes were penetrating. "Did something happen there?"

I nodded. "Maybe I was too sensitive. Too weak. I was uncertain about everything." Marie's inquiry was to be expected. But the thought of revelation crushed me. "It was his tone I think. And the smirk on all their faces when Brian asked me a question. I felt like I was sucker punched. Didn't see it coming. This was near the end of the school year. I still remember exactly what was said. And how it was said. Still can't shake it. So fucking insensitive...and cold." I lowered my head at the bitterness of the memory.

"What did he ask, Gregg?"

"It just came out of nowhere. He asked in front of the whole group, 'So you knocked up your girl?' Just like that...*knocked up*. I hate that phrase." An avalanche of guilt and embarrassment descended upon me. Here I was sitting in a psych room telling my nurse about my teenage secret. Or what I thought was a secret. "And I remember... my insides crumbling in a raging silence. They all laughed out loud. They knew my girlfriend was pregnant. It was like a joke to them. They even knew she was living somewhere in some other state. It was funny to them. Something they could laugh at me about."

"So that's how you found out others knew?" She seemed unmoved. Nothing I told Marie seemed to shock her. I can only imagine the stories she heard during her nursing stint on E2. So I'm sure a teenage pregnancy didn't skyrocket to the top of her list.

"Yeah. That was it." I sensed Marie cared. And that she was concerned. Although I obsessively guarded my story, the more I spoke with her, the more I felt the chains of secrecy being unlocked.

"So you're going to be a father."

"Yeah. If you can call it that."

"I'm not sure if I should say *congratulations.* Probably not the appropriate thing to say if the pregnancy, and everything that followed landed you in E2."

I nodded, glancing at the clock on the wall and wondering how long Marie would stay. But we talked for an hour. I told Marie everything.

"And how did all that go down, Gregg? When did you find out?"

I began to tell my story. "There was a major snowstorm that night. We stood in the middle of New Scotland Avenue. No one was out. No traffic. No other people. Just us standing in the middle of the street in the wind and snow." At this point I wanted to share the events with Marie. I wanted her to know what had happened that led to my inability to cope. "I remember feeling frozen in anger. For weeks she told me her parents were sending her out of state to help her pregnant sister. After that there was tension and sadness whenever we were with each other. I was angry that she was leaving. We were both angry. I mean...

she would have to change schools. To move from her home. To leave our relationship. Just to help her sister? It all seemed unreal. And then she dropped a bomb and said she had to leave tomorrow. We argued. I didn't want her to go. I didn't understand why *she* had to go. She got so angry and kept saying, 'Do you think I want to go? Do you think it is my choice? Do you think I want to leave you!?' She sobbed and started walking up New Scotland Avenue towards her home."

Marie asked, "Did her parents speak to you about her leaving? Did they tell your parents?"

"No. I still remember her slow movements in the snow away from me. That scene hurts when I think about it. You know...that someone I truly cared about was just being sent away? I remember screaming in the middle of the road, 'This is fucking crazy!'"

"Departures in any relationship are difficult, Gregg. And probably more so for teenagers."

"I screamed again as loud as I could. I remember the snow blowing into my mouth. I lost it. She was my age. We were both sixteen. She came from money. I'm talking - *big time real estate money.* Upper class. Private schools for the children. A big home up past St. Peter's Hospital. And I was the milkman's son who lived in the back of a kindergarten building. The wrong side of the tracks to her family. I know I'm rambling now, Marie." I sighed and caught myself squeezing Marie's hand. "I guess I just want to tell you. I remember the wind howling and tree branches cracking. The snow piled up in eerie silence. I thought she was ignoring me as she walked away. Maybe she didn't hear me. So I screamed, 'This is bullshit! Your parents are just trying to get you away from me!'"

Marie stood to adjust the curtain and block the sun glaring into the room. "Did you believe that, Gregg?"

"Yeah. I thought that was true. But I never expected what she yelled back to me."

"You keep saying 'she' and 'her.'" Marie's right hand clutched my chair. "What's your girlfriend's name?"

"That's not important." I may have relinquished my shield of protection but I was going to protect hers. "Then, maybe twenty yards up the road she turned back towards me and yelled, 'You think it's bullshit, Gregg?' I could tell she was crying. 'You don't want to hear the bullshit anymore?' And the words that changed my life forever tumbled out of her mouth, 'Do you really want to know? No more bullshit. She isn't the one who is pregnant. I'm pregnant.' And then she turned and ran out of my life. She ran up New Scotland Avenue to her home behind St. Catherine's Church."

"I don't know what to say. Gregg. That is such a sad story. For both of you." Marie checked her watch, sat back in her chair, and sighed. "Brother Leo failing you...and then the insensitive and hurtful question from your classmate. Before that, for months, you knew about the pregnancy and kept it to yourself. I guess I understand now why you didn't want to go back to VI. Did your girlfriend really go to another state?"

"I think so. Never saw her again. One big fucking lie her parents tried to play out. Sorry for my language. Get her out of town, put the baby up for adoption, and then just go on with their uppity lives."

"You didn't see your girlfriend at all during the pregnancy?"

"See her? I wasn't supposed to even know she was pregnant. No. I never saw her. And I never saw the baby. I didn't even know where she went or where the baby was born." I felt floodgates to my heart had broken and the words were flowing out painfully, "Sometimes, like at night when I was drinking too much and hoping to pass out, I thought it was a bad dream; a nightmare. My best friend, Lemily, once he found out - he knew her family - he told me he thought her parents sent her away to get rid of the kid. An abortion somewhere. He said, 'Think about it, Gregg - your folks are like parents to all of us. But her old man and old lady couldn't let their daughter have a baby by a milkman's son. It would ruin their name in the neighborhood and their business'."

"And you never got to speak to her after she left? I mean how did you even find out if your child was born or if your friend Lemily was right?"

"Phone calls. Weekly calls we arranged that no one was to know about. I got a letter weeks after she left. There was a phone number and she told me what day to call and what time. And that she would answer. She told me to call from a payphone and to bring a lot of change with me. So I knew it was a long distance call. That part of the story was true. She *was* sent away. She told me the date to make my first call and I did."

I'm not sure why, but for the first time I realized the gloom of the environment at E2. The walls were plain, undecorated, and the gray paint was peeling. There was no bedside lighting, only a switch to turn on the main overhead light. The small TV hung from a black metal ceiling mount. And the bed frames and chairs were old gray metal; cold and uninviting accented by a barren coldness. And, of course, a squeaky old food table where I kept a notebook and a book of poems by Leonard Cohen. Most of the time in my room I listened to my transistor.

I hated being here and survived only because of my time with Marie and LeRoy.

Marie continued, "Did you write back when you got her letter or wait to call her?"

"Couldn't write back. There was no return address. Top secret," I smirked. "I was kept completely out of the loop. At least we spoke on the phone once a week. But I could tell she was even nervous about our calls. But we had our plan. And I guess it worked because no one ever found out we were talking with each other."

"Plan?"

"Yeah. Wherever they sent her, she had access to a payphone at a designated time and I called exactly when she told me. There's a phone booth on Madison Avenue a few blocks up from where I lived. Outside the A&P. The store is right across from the police station."

"I know exactly where you mean." Marie said. "That's where I get my groceries - at that A&P."

I nodded my head at the awkward image that flushed through my mind. I smiled. "That's crazy."

"What do you mean?"

"Like I know you *now*, Marie." I realized this was the first time I called her by her name. "Being locked up here. But we could have seen each other by the A&P over the summer and fall. That's crazy, isn't it?"

"I guess so, Gregg. I know the phone booth you are talking about. Is that where you called from?"

"Yeah. I would get there like ten minutes early and pretend I was making a call by looking through the pages of the chained up phone book. I didn't want anyone to be in the booth when I was supposed to call. I was so worried about not connecting. Not finding out about what was going on. Missing out on some news. But that was it...our phone calls. I never got that much information. I don't know...it was so messed up. Long distance phone partners. I was so nervous just dialing the numbers. I messed up the numbers so many times. I worried something would go wrong with the call - or that something was wrong with her. Standing in the phone booth I felt like I didn't matter. That I was nobody. The father of a baby...but nobody. Not worth even being told what was going on. I guess the easy choice for her parents was to eliminate me. And if you had their money, you could do that."

I felt Marie's hand rubbing on my arm. "Thanks for telling me, Gregg."

"Yeah." I took a deep breath to regroup. "I would get so angry at myself for being helpless. A child of mine was being born somewhere and I was completely cut out of the picture. I felt so insignificant. We never talked about what was actually happening: boy - girl - name - or even if Lemily's suspicion was correct. Just typical BS conversations: 'How are you doing? Feeling OK?' But at least we talked. My life became the A&P phone booth and our calls. As it got closer to the November due date, I just crashed. I couldn't go to school. Couldn't be around anyone. Nothing seemed to matter. That's when I dropped out of Albany High School. I couldn't relate to anyone anymore. What was going on in my life was so different from what my friends were into. All I was able to do with them was drink and get screwed up any way possible. I knew I was out of control and fucking myself up. But I didn't care. My friends were drinking all the time, doing all kinds of drugs - speed, acid, pot, downers...and it was easy for me to do the same. When I got screwed up, I didn't think about what was really going on in my life."

"Getting screwed up like that got rid of the pain." Marie acknowledged. "I'm sure you felt like that was a quick way to escape, Gregg. But it was just a temporary fix. Getting messed up didn't help you deal with everything. You got rid of the pain that night... but you also got yourself into the hospital. Do you know what happened to your baby?"

"*My baby?*" I smirked. "A baby girl. That's what I was told. I was told she was put up for adoption. I don't know where she is or who she lives with now. Just that she was never to be seen by me. That was the plan all along. I don't know how my girlfriend dealt with everything. I know she didn't want to give the baby up. I couldn't deal with that and I can't even imagine the pain she felt. I mean she saw our baby. Held our baby. But that was it. I never saw a picture of her. Yeah...'*my baby.*' Doesn't sound real, does it, Marie?"

CHAPTER NINE

In the Red Zone

How does it feel to be on your own
with no direction home

— Bob Dylan —

During my last two days at E2 I was in a tailspin mentally and emotionally. Anxious. Depressed. Scared. Happy. Uncertain. Directionless. I hated being inside this place. But ironically, only dread filtered through me as my release date neared. I was flushed with anxiety wondering what awaited me on the outside.

LeRoy was discharged on my sixth day; one day before my stint in the hospital was to end. A nurse escorted him into my room to say goodbye. He clutched his discharge papers in his left hand and waved them at me as he spoke. "This is it, kid. I'm outta here. Best never come back. I'm gonna try my damn best. I got a gift for you." He took his drumsticks out of his back pocket and handed them to me." For the time LeRoy and I resided on E2, we became *real friends.* "You outta here tomorrow, ain't you?"

"Yeah." I smiled. "Unless I fuck someone up with these sticks." The nurse was not very fond of my comment looking at me with her mean nurse eyes. "Whenever I look at them, LeRoy, I'll think of you."

LeRoy leaned towards me. His massive hand took a firm hold of the back of my neck. "I ain't kidding 'bout what I told you, kid..." He shook my neck gently but authoritatively. "You gots people who care 'bout you - friends, family. If I ever see you back in this place, I'm gonna kick the shit outta you."

We shook hands and shared a final laugh together. Sadness engulfed me as LeRoy exited my room. And my life.

More frequent visits from Marie offset my loneliness. Shorter visits time wise. But more drop-ins to check in on me.

Marie seemed different. Did she feel like she now entered a *do not trespass zone* of my life? Did she worry that what I revealed to her should have been told to the medical team during counseling sessions and not to a student nurse?

I wondered if Marie felt the secrets divulged to her were too embedded in the darkness of my past? Maybe she no longer wanted to escort me from the abyss I was trying to climb out of.

I became more engaged in my sessions with Dr. Shrink. I went to my appointments with an *end in sight* attitude that allowed me to be more open and responsive.

My doctor informed me about a discharge meeting scheduled with my parents to discuss my plans and the support network he hoped would be there once I was home. In my last two meetings with my psychiatrist, I told him about the reasons for my crash and how I ended up in E2. Before I opened up, I thought he only knew the overdose details and self-destructive behavior that brought on my admission to the hospital. "I've been in contact with your psychiatrist who you were seeing during the summer, Dr. Anolik."

So there it was. He already knew. Either from my parents. Or from Dr. Anolik. Who knows what I signed away for myself on the night I was admitted to the hospital? But for some reason I no longer cared who knew what about me. I was ready to be open and to welcome the support from the doctors, my family, and my friends. I wanted to put my life back together. I wanted help in dealing with what had happened. In the past year, I had lost control of every other part of my life. Now, I only wanted to find a path to move forward. I wanted *myself to be myself again.* But there was an awkwardness at this appointment with Dr. Shrink. He was hinting at things that were even unknown to Dr. Anolik. I had stopped my appointments with that psychiatrist months before the birth of my baby.

"Yeah. Dr. Anolik. I started seeing him in the springtime. Could you understand him when he talked?" I deflected with a smile.

"Yes, Gregory. I know him well. Professionally. You get accustomed to the German accent. A brilliant man."

"Well...I think I only understood half of what he said to me. So I guess he only helped me get half better."

Dr. Shrink wasn't one to smile. But a hint of a smile came across his bearded face. "Gregory, you have grown emotionally and psychologically during your time in the hospital. I know you detest being here, but I believe your stay has helped you gain perspective. I think you will be more resilient. And definitely less self-destructive. You are much stronger. Even now, just in our conversation, your sarcasm is rooted in confidence and not just as a way to deflect anger."

"I never heard that one before, Doc." I reflected on the connection between sarcasm and confidence.

Dr. Shrink continued. "Many people deflect through sarcasm. But others use sarcasm for humor demonstrating confidence. It depends on if your intent is to hurt or belittle - or to bring a smile."

"I guess. I think I understand."

"For several months over the summer and until being admitted to the hospital, you were confronted with many challenges that created conflict and confusion for someone your age: isolation, loneliness, confusion, self-doubt, and fear brought about by an unexpected pregnancy." He tapped his desk as he stated each characteristic like he was dealing in a game of five card stud. "Subsequently, you descended into a realm of substance and alcohol abuse."

I nodded in agreement with the doctor's assessment.

"I believe you felt your world had abandoned you. But at this point, whether or not that is true, is not the issue now. You will never be able to gain a complete understanding of the motives of everyone involved. You cannot cut through that past to find out because it is not exclusively your past. Although some parts of that history you are responsible for, through both your actions and reactions. And those parts will continue to confront and challenge your resilience."

"No shit." I think I was sidestepping the "responsible" part of Dr. Shrink's analysis. Playing the victim was always much easier. "I knew so little about what was going on...and could never get answers. And like you said, I can't cut through that bullshit now." An echo from a session with Dr. Anolik caused me to smirk.

"What are you smiling about, Gregory?" I wish Dr. Shrink would just call me Gregg.

"Just remembering an appointment with Dr. Anolik. During the summer. I remember being so angry at everything and everyone. The lies and falsehoods. And he said - he was always so calm, even when I was flipping out - he said, 'You have to stop trying to fight through this.' He said, 'You cannot manipulate the past. You can only control how you manage the past. Fair or unfair - you are not in control of the past. Your past is like a piece of leather. You can't cut through the leather of your past.' Sounds like the same thing you're telling me now."

"Dr. Anolik was correct. But you have kept fighting; trying to cut through. But in this bout, your punches are meaningless. And you keep trying to cut through what is impossible to cut through. And we are here now - in the present. Not to ignore but to confront, deal with, and move along from what happened. Your stay at E2 is almost over. You go home with your parents when you are discharged. And you will be without your child. The fact you now must endure to go forward, is that your girlfriend was sent away to give birth and the baby was put up for adoption." My face started to burn. My fists clenched. "That is the story of your life, *your life.* The fact that you spent a week here is testimony that you could not endure that reality. And so you ended up in E2. But now, I think..."

Without hesitation, I slammed my fist on the table and interrupted angrily, "How do you know that!? That the baby was put up for adoption? I never told you. Did my parents tell you?"

"How I know is not important. Unless that is not what happened." Dr. Shrink was the one doing the sidestepping now. "How you internalize that truth, that reality, and what you do with yourself to transcend your dilemma, is what is important now. For today. For tomorrow. And for your future. That is what is important as you prepare for your discharge."

"Bullshit!" My body quivered and my face tightened with exasperation. My session with Dr. Shrink concluded in silence.

A few hours later, Marie walked into my room with my medications. She gestured for me to sit in one of the extra chairs. "We just had a team meeting. Your doctor asked me to check in on you and report back to him. He said you were very upset when you left your appointment."

I stepped down from my bed and sat in the chair across from Marie. Sullen and unusually disinterested. "Yeah. Same bullshit seems to keep going down. People know things about me and I don't even know how they found out. I got pissed at him. I just feel like things are done and said behind my back. Maybe it doesn't matter, I mean what he said was the truth about me fucking up my life."

"The baby and the adoption?" Marie asked.

"Yeah. I mean what he said wasn't a bunch of lies. But I don't know how much my parents are telling him. Or maybe things are spilling out here from friends and other people who visit. I probably sound paranoid."

Marie pushed my medications across the bedside table towards me. She poured a glass of water. "I'm sorry, Gregg." She was uncomfortable and struggled for words. "I...ughhh...I..." She was nervous and hesitant to finish her statement.

"No!" I glared at my nurse. Disbelief rattled me. "You told him!?"

"Please, Gregg. Please listen to me. There was just a feeling with the medical team that they were getting nowhere with you. No one could get through to you. They believe your treatment was only surface level. No one knew what had driven you to the breaking point. There is not a single person on the floor here who didn't want to help you, Gregg. Everyone thinks you are getting better. And that we're helping you. But no one knows what we are helping you with and that you are still one misstep away from another crash. No one knew. Except me."

"I can't believe this. It was you. I really can't trust anyone!"

"When you told me the things that happened, all that you were dealing with...I know you probably hate me for this...I know I violated our trust...but I like you, Gregg. I like you a lot. And I just wanted you to get all the help you could while you are here. Please, Gregg. Yes. I told your doctor. But only because I thought it would help you. The only reason, Gregg. I swear. The only reason."

What I believed was my surreptitious being was a secret no more. I was shaken. I felt violated. Marie was the last person I expected would rap about my past. I trusted her so much. "Did they plant you here, Marie?" My anger turned hostile. "Your kindness. Your frequent visits. Were our talks just a game? This is so fucking far out!" I felt I was losing it again.

"No." She responded assertively. "I was not planted to get information from you. If I was asked to do that, I would have said no. It's just that when you opened up and told me everything...I care so much about you...I just wanted you to get help. That's all, Gregg. I just want you to be at peace. I never told you this, but one afternoon I stopped in and you were asleep and you were calling out the names of girls. What was that about? Baby names you thought of? It was so sad knowing your story. But then I would go to a team meeting, and we would discuss progress with patients, and no one had a clue about you...no one even knew why you were here except that you drank too much and took too many pills. But that was just a scrap of information on the intake papers. But I knew there was so much more, and closing down on everyone wasn't going to help."

My glare intensified. "But that wasn't your choice to tell, Marie." Distrust consumed me. "So you told everyone?"

"I only told Doctor Adair. I asked for a meeting with him and told him. Only him, Gregg. I'm certain no one else here knows. I told him how conflicted I was about talking to him and how I felt like I was breaking a trust. I know your doctor isn't one to reveal a confidential meeting with me."

"But you did." There was no forgiveness in my voice.

"I know. I know, Gregg. But I worried you were being discharged in just a few days and no one was addressing what was really going on inside you. And how everything just exploded and landed you in the hospital. I was worried you would end up back here. I told him in strict confidence. I did, Gregg. I don't think you should worry that your psychiatrist will say anything to anyone."

"Was that the same '*strict confidence*' I thought I had with you, Marie?" Only now did I understand Doctor Adair's (AKA Dr. Shrink) message on sarcasm. But this time, my intent was to hurt.

"Gregg, please believe me."

I shook my head in a furious gesture of disbelief. I put the pills into my mouth and swallowed them with a large gulp of water. "Man...I just can't believe this crap is going down. Even in this place. I thought..."

Marie interrupted. "I know. I am very sorry. I was so conflicted. I just wanted you to get yourself together and get helped before you left here. Don't for a second think that it doesn't bother me that I did this. I wish I was never in this position. I told your doctor I even wished I was not your nurse. Gregg, try to believe me. I mean this so much. I thought I was doing the right thing to help you. And that is all I wanted to do. Hate me all you want, but telling Dr. Adair came from my heart."

Moments of silence descended between us like barbed wire.

Slowly, the rage I felt inside was erased because I believed Marie. Besides, what did it matter? What she told Dr. Adair was the truth. She wasn't lying about me. Our silence seemed to turn the volume on the radio louder. Ironically, Johnny Rivers was singing, "The Poor Side of Town."

Wiping away the glare from my eyes I feigned a smile. "I think I want to be by myself, Marie. I understand. Thanks for being honest. It's just a lot to take in. You know I have a lot of trust issues...and this doesn't help. I just need to mellow out. Maybe when your shift is over you could stop back before you leave?"

CHAPTER TEN

My Discharge - The Milk Truck Is Waiting

The final forming of a person's character lies in their own hands.

— Anne Frank —

After breakfast I went to my morning appointment with Dr. Adair.

Once LeRoy was discharged the rest of my time in the hospital consisted of group sessions, visits with Marie, writing, chatting up visitors, and my appointments with Dr. Adair.

My cousin stopped by. His visit was an unexpected but welcomed surprise. And my friends arrived again the night before my release. They were always so loud and insensitive. To them hospital protocols were merely polysyllabic words that did not apply. When the Madison Avenue and Ridgefield Park crew showed up, I'm sure the staff felt like they were under siege; an insurrection.

Nurse Meanie, the same nurse who booted Bucky out, was on duty. Her unwavering and stern authoritative attitude was a good thing for the hospital when my friends visited. She held firm to the rule limiting visitors to enter E2. This was Nurse Meanie's rule for law and order. My friends scheduled themselves throughout the visiting hours arriving at the hospital in a group but taking the elevator to E2 at different times. Word got back to me after visiting hours that there was quite a raucous in the hospital lounge while my friends were awaiting their turn. I was not surprised.

I had my final time with Dr. Shrink....I mean Dr. Adair. There was no reason for me to be a wiseass about him any longer. At this appointment I finally noticed all the degrees and awards that hung on his office wall. I was impressed by the display of professional accomplishments. My attitude towards my psychiatrist changed in my final days. I became appreciative of his efforts to help put me back together. He *knew my story.* Marie had told him. Even with my story revealed, I actually felt relief...and even strength. I was no longer weighed down by the ball and chain burden of my past history.

I also realized that Dr. Adair never judged me. And I welcomed that. I didn't feel insignificant with him. I felt he recognized that I really wanted to climb out from the mire of a teenage crisis that had become my life this past year. With Dr. Adair there was no labeling of fault or blame. Several times he would begin our sessions establishing his motif, "So Gregory, the questions we will focus on again are: where are you *at* today? And where do you want your head to be tomorrow?"

I picked up on the psychological game: regardless of how I answered the question, my response required that I take ownership. My life. No one is at fault. No one to blame. Just my life. Pull up the bootstraps and take ownership.

My Dad was in the hallway during my last session. He met with Dr. Adair before my appointment. I was surprised at how quickly my release was processed. Maybe I figured I did a lot of crap to get into E2, so there would be a lot of crap to do when I got out.

"Well, Gregg...this is it." Dr. Adair handed me several documents. "We just need you to sign some papers. Your father signed the necessary parent signatures. "I'm sure you were glad to see him?" I flashed back to a familiar paper signing scene a week ago.

"You have no clue how glad I am, Doctor."

"Take your time reading over the release forms before you sign and I will summarize each page for you." He handed me his clipboard as he explained each page. "I know you had an issue with what you signed when you came here. Those documents closed the door behind you. These papers are opening the door for you to leave."

I didn't take my time reading through the pages but I listened to each summary and signed quickly. I trusted Dr. Adair. "These don't seem complicated." I signed the last sheet without reading the document. "Easier for me to sign out than to sign in." I started to realize that I survived my time on E2 and I was being released.

Dr. Adair observed. "I'm sensing anxiousness, Gregg."

"Anxious? I'll probably scream when I get outside."

Dr. Adair leaned back in his massively padded leather chair and sighed. I handed the clipboard back to my doctor after signing all the papers. "It is important to remember, Gregg, that you don't get to go through life in a positive light without having faith that you can trust people. And you will never find those people unless you are willing to take the risk. This morning I called Dr. Anolik. I scheduled an appointment next week for you. I want you to follow up with him regularly. And take any medications Dr. Anolik prescribes."

I nodded. "I will, Doctor." I agreed, not knowing if I was telling the truth.

Dr. Adair stood, "You deserve a life better than the one you gave to yourself this year."

Ouch. There was fault and blame in that statement but I wasn't playing the victim now. I sensed his message of individual responsibility. "I don't know what is next. But I know I don't want this." With my thumb I pointed over my shoulder to the patient wing of E2.

"Remember, Gregg, just signing these papers and walking out of here doesn't guarantee a positive future. You will always have work to do. Life is fluid...with many transitions and challenges. How you handle each one is what will shape the rest of your life."

"Well...I'm ready." I wanted so badly to see my Dad and to walk out of the hospital. "I'm ready." I pushed myself up from the chair. "The only thing I know for sure is I ain't coming back here. Do you know if Marie is working today?"

"She is not on the schedule. But she was going to try to stop by before you left."

I didn't want to leave without seeing Marie. But there would be no holding me back from the exit door. I worried I would never see my nurse again once I walked out of the hospital. There was a firestorm of mixed emotions: happy and anxious to get out of the hospital, but sad and unsettled that today was the end of my friendship with my nurse. I wanted to say goodbye to Marie.

I picked up my blue gym bag where I packed my clothing, my notebook, and LeRoy's drumsticks. I opened the door and saw the thick shoulders and hunched posture of my father that earned him the nickname I gave to him, *The Bear.* What I didn't see immediately as the door opened, was Marie. She was standing near my father and talking to him.

"I'm so glad you made it over, Marie. I asked Dr. Adair if you were working today."

Marie lifted a gift bag from her pocketbook. "I wasn't going to let that happen. I got something for you but I don't want you to open it until you are home."

At this point I was engulfed in contradictory feelings of joy and regret. My father was here to take me home. And Marie was here to say goodbye.

"Thank you. For everything. Last night I was thinking...you're just like the girls who are my friends on Madison Avenue. Friends. You meant so much to me while I was here, Marie."

"Just keep your heart open, Gregg." We hugged each other gently and she whispered, "There are plenty of Maries out there. Give them a chance and let them in."

Marie pushed away gently from me but kept her hands on my arms. We were silent for a moment and then my father interrupted, "You ready to get out of here?" My father was never one for socializing. "The truck is running. Nice to meet you, Nurse." He shook Marie's hand. My Dad was the least formal person I knew but he maintained some traditional gestures that didn't match his gruffness. He was never the sensitive type. That was my mother.

"I won't forget you, Marie."

"And I won't forget you." We embraced again quickly for the final time. She whispered, "Please take care of yourself, Gregg."

Outside, despite the cold autumnal air, the sun seemed unusually bright. My Dad created a special milk truck parking spot for himself. I never had the parental connections money could buy, but I had the milkman connections my father utilized to park close to the exit door.

There was no passenger seat in the truck. My father stacked two empty milk crates on top of each other and that was my seat. Climbing into the truck, I sat down and flashed back to my earlier years when I would help my father on his milk route. But today, despite the discomfort of the seats, I felt like I was getting limousine service away from the hospital and back to my home.

CHAPTER ELEVEN

The Making of a Teacher

And time waits for no one,
and it won't wait for me

— Jagger/Richards —

My journey to my teaching career was an uncertain passage through a swampland of irresponsible actions and misguided choices. I struggled through the quicksand of being a dangerously at-risk teenager during the concluding years of my adolescence.

Final cost of my poor decisions? I had put my life two years behind my "normal" classmates, most of whom sailed through their existence into adulthood. Dropping out of high school created the first year of my sabbatical. And I lost a second year when I withdrew from college to pay off gambling debts with my student loan. When I reflect on those lost years, my initial thought is, "what an asshole". But as I worked on this memoir, I realized the unique and powerful sense of self-worth and resilience that comes with putting scattered pieces of a life back together.

I'm not much of a religious person. I mean, I do believe. But formal religious practice ended for me after my altar boy days at VI. Still, having been glued to the rearview mirror of my life to write this book, I believe some higher power kept me grounded and guided me throughout my career.

Not all aspects of my life were a blessing and success after my departure from E2. The evil jujuman of future mistakes found an easy target in me. Maybe all that is for another memoir. This one is about my recovery and my career as an educator.

In hindsight, teaching for me went far beyond the exchange of subject knowledge. Often, when asked about working with troubled students my entire career, I resorted to a catch-all response, "I feel I am as much their counselor, social worker, family court advocate, and life coach as I am their English teacher."

Close to my heart, I kept the scarred memory of my descent into the abyss during my latter teen years. After my discharge from E2 I purchased a St. Jude medal; the patron saint of lost causes. I continue to wear the medal. Someone had watched over me.

I endured the guilt and pain of bringing a child into this world who was secretly put up for adoption. But forever, I will carry the memory of being a father who wasn't supposed to exist.

I transcended a stage in my youth of excessive drug and alcohol abuse.

I survived a weeklong stay in a psychiatric unit of a hospital.

I got my high school diploma and received a college degree in education.

I became a teacher of at-risk teenagers for thirty-five years.

A few years after I retired, I was sitting at the Fountain Restaurant in Albany for a pizza and a few pints. A former high school classmate recognized me. We were almost five decades removed from our high school days. He stood looking down at me where I sat in a booth and nodded recognition.

"Gregor," my teenage nickname, "Recognize me? Mikey...from Madison Avenue. Remember?"

After he introduced himself by name, I did remember. I stood. We shook hands.

"Mikey...how have you been? I heard you stayed in the Army and then moved out of state."

"Yeah. Didn't know what else to do with my life so I stayed on. Vietnam, man. But I'm out now and still in one piece."

"What about you, Gregor?" Mikey asked. "I never kept in touch with anyone back here. What the fuck did you end up doing with your life?"

"I was a teacher. Thirty-five years."

"You!?" Mikey said in disbelief. "A teacher? No way. You were such a fuckup when we were teenagers."

I had a flashback to my students.

Teenage fuckups just like their teacher. No wonder I lasted thirty-five years teaching at-risk students.

Been there - Taught that.

CHAPTER TWELVE

The Slow Climb Up

I've been down so goddamn long
that it looks like up to me

— Jim Morrison —

On the ride home in my Dad's milk truck, driving up New Scotland Avenue and over Partridge Street to Madison Avenue, I realized I never said the word *goodbye* to Marie. I'm glad.

I never saw Marie again. In memory, I will forever cherish our connection and the time we shared during my stay in E2. Sometimes, when I'm thinking of Marie during drink-thoughts, I smile and say to myself, "Girls, they just have a way of disappearing from my life."

The months after my discharge were filled with fear and anxiety. A lethal mix of emotions. I was living under an avalanche of existential questions that I could not answer. I was both alone and lonely. My friends were either at school, working, or in the military. I filled the hours of my days helping on the milk route, working with my Dad on his side maintenance jobs, sending my poetry to literary magazines, and hanging out at Knapp's Tavern waiting for my friends to arrive. Eighteen was the drinking age during my teenage years. But then, at Knapp's Tavern, most of us turned eighteen at fifteen or sixteen.

Next door to Knapp's, the cops and politicians frequented Joe's Delicatessen. On many nights, Madison Avenue, between Ontario and Partridge Street, was lined with police cars, Cadillacs, and even limousines. The plebians, my friends and I, stood at Knapp's front window and watched the parade of money we would never have, cruising into Joe's.

During this period of life, trying to kick my way forward, a poem of mine was published in a local weekly. My friend Smitty told me that Sister Joyce at VI saw my poem and wanted me to come to her class and talk about writing. I have no memory of what I said in the class when I visited. I do remember Sister Joyce handing out copies of the free weekly to her students.

I remember reading the poem to the class and answering some questions. But that was it. I don't remember the questions. I don't remember my answers. I don't remember the reaction of the students. I don't remember any discussions. But I do remember what Sister Joyce said to me when the bell rang, "Thank you for visiting, Gregg. I think my students related to your poem. And you have a confident and appealing presence in front of a classroom."

That, I will remember. I walked out of the enormous brick structure of Vincentian Institute and onto Madison Avenue feeling like a prodigal son returning to so many positive years of my life.

I thought to myself, *I'm OK. I did it.*

I returned to the school I swore would never see my face again. And I was OK. And the school was OK with me.

The experience in Sister Joyce's creative writing class along with her positive comments, provided me with a sense of validation. But I am certain my presentation was likely incredibly sophomoric.

Yet I felt I belonged. I felt significant. I felt purpose.

That spring afternoon, in Sister Joyce's eleventh grade class, the proverbial light switch turned on.

I wanted to go back to school. Get my high school diploma. Go to college. And who knows, maybe become a teacher.

CHAPTER THIRTEEN

The Prodigal Son Returns

I was so much older then
I'm younger than that now

— Bob Dylan —

I returned to VI in September 1968. From my first day back at my home school, I felt strange. I struggled with an intense sense of not belonging. These were not my classmates I went to school with since kindergarten. Those classmates graduated last June. I felt so different. Out of place. Everything that went on at the school seemed childish, almost immature. And now I was part of that scene as a returning high school senior. Again.

I ignored the behind-the-back comments and rumors:

He's probably still on drugs.

He came back just to deal drugs.

He was even in the nuthouse.

He'll just drop out again.

Thankfully, I never heard a comment about pregnancy, fatherhood, or a baby from any faculty member in the building.

I am certain my teachers knew about my previous year. The news did not have to travel far. I lived near the Brother's of Holy Cross residence on Madison Avenue. And the Sisters of Mercy convent, where I was the early morning altar boy for the nuns, was the next block over on Morris Street. But the issue of why I had dropped out of school was never mentioned by the adults at VI.

My interactions with my English teacher, Brother David Warnke, convinced me that even without mentioning anything, he knew the cause of my *sabbatical.* His class was the last period of the school day. I remember a meeting with him after school.

David was a tall man with an overdose of dandruff on the shoulders of his black Brothers' suit. In class, he intimidated his students with his literary genius and massive vocabulary. Never had I met a man as well read as Brother David. He was an intellectual with the soul of a beat poet. Sensitive. And down to earth. Despite Brother David's commitment to his religious order, he was unlike all the other Brothers of Holy Cross who taught at the school. He was street-smart with a *world of experiences* from his travels. A devout believer who questioned conformity. A Notre Dame graduate who later in the school year told me he purposely spent the hours of home football games in the library. *Go Irish!*

"Just wanted to check in with you, Gregg." His jacket was decorated with chalk markings from his blackboard lectures. But he didn't care. "I can tell your mind is drifting on me sometimes during class. You seem to have a fondness for the window overlooking the basketball court across the street."

"Sorry." I shrugged, casually admitting to my misdeed. I tried to leave my defiance behind at E2. This was Brother David's first year at VI and I liked that he proudly stood apart from his colleagues. "I do drift sometimes. That park is like one of my homes away from home."

"I heard you had a year off. Took a sabbatical."

"Sabbatical?"

"Yes. Like a leave of absence. And after spending all those years of education at VI, you decided to branch out in your intellectual growth." David was also witty and sarcastic.

Smiling, I responded, “I like that word. Sabbatical. Thanks for putting my dropping out in that context.”

“Anyone would find it difficult to get back into the groove after a year out. To have a sympatico relationship with the other students here.”

Here we go, I thought. Brother Polysyllabic. “Difficult to be *what?*”

“Sympatico.”

“And that means?” Brother David knew I had no clue what he was saying.

“I’ll let you figure that out. I’ll make sure sympatico is on the vocabulary quiz on Friday.” I watched him write the word on a tablet. “I asked you to stay after because there are times I think your headspace is cluttered. You’re not catching what is going on in class. And I want you to know I am aware. And one more thing…I enjoy reading your journals. A very different read for me instead of reading the usual writings about school dances, breakups, curfews, and outcomes of sporting events.”

I smiled awkwardly. My journals were heartfelt but also sad. “Thanks.”

October lingered and stalled like a bad dream I couldn’t shake. Flashbacks to my time in E2, and the reasons I ended up in the hospital, frequented my thoughts. I missed my connection with Marie. And LeRoy. And even Dr. Adair. But those memories paled in the thoughts of my adopted child. More troubling were my feelings of insignificance. Like figuratively only being a father. I knew what I was doing to myself mentally and emotionally with my inability to compartmentalize my thoughts. But I couldn’t escape the haunting echo of Nietzche’s words I first heard in Brother David’s class, “When you stare into the abyss, the abyss will gaze into you.”

In the hours after school, I didn’t “stare into the abyss.” I descended into the abyss. I was drinking more and smoking pot. My friends were accommodating. At the *Down on the corner* park someone was always willing to escape and get wasted. And I did just that...with Lemily, or Percy, or Sharon, or Bucky.

CHAPTER FOURTEEN

My High School Graduation

I been in the right place
But it must have been the wrong time

— Dr. John —

I finished high school at Vincentian. Thirteen years of my life at VI, beginning in Kindergarten and concluding with my graduation. And now the doors to Vincentian would finally close for me in June.

Besides Brother David, other teachers helped me through the school year - my music teacher, Mrs. Itzkow, my Contemporary Studies teacher, Sister Joyce, and my Business teacher, Brother Alfred.

Mrs. Itzkow was a small, forever positive Jewish woman teaching in a Catholic school. Not music lessons. Her class was a historical perspective of music. Her passion was classical music. On Fridays, we were allowed to bring in records we wanted to hear. She was amazingly tolerant of the folk and rock music her students preferred.

I enjoyed her class, but I suspect I didn't endear myself to my classmates when I showed up with my Bob Dylan albums.

Several years after graduation, when I was teaching at Berkshire Farm for Boys, a residential school for adjudicated delinquents in Canaan, NY, I was reacquainted with Mrs. Itzkow. I walked into an Irish import shop on Colvin Avenue in Albany and Mrs. Itzkow was behind the counter. We remembered each other immediately. I was surprised to learn she owned the Irish import store. In my small world, a Jewish woman teaching music in a Catholic school was strange. And now Mrs. Itzkow owned an Irish gift store. But she was a special woman. If only the world was more populated with the likes of Rose Itzkow, we would be blessed with a much kinder and safer existence.

My Contemporary Studies class focused on analyzing important current events and sharing our opinions on the topics. Being the late sixties, the media was a daily explosion of memorable news. I excelled in the class. No doubt reading Brother David's copy of the *NY Times* every day put me at an "information" advantage in the class.

I was more opinionated than my classmates. When we talked about the landing on the moon, Sister Joyce went on about all the future possibilities that will evolve as a result of the historical event. I wasn't interested. Hard enough to keep my head together on earth without going into space. She called on me to share my thoughts, "I don't care if the whole school moves up to the moon. I'm staying right here on this planet."

Sometimes, instead of a news event, Sister Joyce asked us to share what we did on the weekend. My stories were always different. I had friends in serious adult life situations far beyond the daily drama of high school. Friends being sent off to Vietnam, a few in detox facilities, some already with families, and a few in Albany County Jail. Drunks. Soldiers in an unknown land. Drug abusers. And all of them in a daily struggle to find some meaning to their lives.

During one class, Sister Joyce asked her students to share a story about someone we knew who dealt with addiction and alcoholism, "But no last names, change the first name if you want, and we keep our conversations in this class confidential." That academic task was an easy challenge for me.

I shared my story about Timmy the Drunk and our football team, The Ridgefield Raiders. No one on our team had the self-discipline to play school sports. My classmates knew about the Raiders. We had a reputation. We always won. We played tackle football without equipment at Ridgefield Park. We played teams from other neighborhoods and communities like Whitehall Road, Colonie, New Scotland Avenue, and North Albany. The losing team paid for the keg of beer. The winning team drank for free. We drank a lot of beer for free.

Timmy was one of our best players, running back and linebacker. But he often spent Saturday night at the Division One Police Station. The weekend ritual was: Timmy would drink. Timmy would get crazy drunk. Timmy would be taken away by the cops for public intoxication.

But we needed Timmy for our games on Sunday.

On game day, our team of hellbent hooligans would meet at Knapp's Tavern. Someone would break the news that Timmy was in lockup again, and we immediately started a collection to pay the fine to get Timmy released from Division One.

We needed Timmy on the field, not in jail. Timmy was that good. When we had both Timmy and Rudy in the backfield, The Ridgefield Raiders had two massive, fearless, hungover, brutal monsters running the ball against youngsters.

There was always extra motivation to win. *We had to win.* We had handed over our money to the Timmy the Drunk fund. We couldn't lose. Once we spent our money to bail Timmy out of jail, we didn't have the money to buy the keg of beer.

I am certain our teacher was looking for stories of the horrors and tragedies of alcohol and drug abuse. But I thought my Timmy the Drunk story was noteworthy. And I actually think Sister Joyce enjoyed the tale. The class laughed. Sister Joyce smiled.

My business teacher, Brother Alfred, was one of my favorite instructors. He was a small man who projected a *don't mess with me* reputation. He made certain his students could see his Popeye muscles bulging out from his black Brothers of Holy Cross short sleeve shirt. Corporal punishment was never an issue at Catholic schools in the sixties. Corporal punishment *was* the Catholic School at the time. The beatings inflicted on some students were so savage, the phrase corporal punishment minimized the physical reprimands often dished out.

I never witnessed Brother Alfred's fierce discipline upon a student. His reputation was solidified before my return to VI. But I am certain that reputation alone controlled student behavior during his classes. His methodology was militaristic with drills and practice, drills and practice, but that teaching style served me well in his classes.

I took both Business Math and Accounting with Brother Alfred. The rebel in me found the black and white rigidity of the business world incongruent with my lifestyle and image. My interests were in the arts. Especially creative writing. I fancied myself a wordsmith, even though mastery of business formulas and calculations came naturally to me. In my Accounting class, my grade was one hundred percent for all four quarters and I capped that off by acing the final exam.

CHAPTER FIFTEEN

Closing Out My Senior Year

To live is to suffer
To survive is to find some meaning in life

— *Nietchze* —

After four months I realized I made the right decision to return to VI. Even though there was an obvious, and often irritating disconnect with my classmates, there was also an understanding support system with the staff at Vincentian Institute.

I still had appointments with Dr. Anolik and there were still prescriptions to balance my moods and keep me in check. But I wanted to stop seeing my psychiatrist. I felt I had become resilient and getting much better at sorting myself out. I was aware of my emotional triggers. Besides, I also felt guilty about the doctor's fee that my parents paid for each session.

I tried to offset the psychiatry costs by helping my father on his Norman's Kill Dairy milk route. And I also helped him with his maintenance job at the VI elementary school. And I worked with my Dad on his side jobs, washing windows and walls (with his *secret solution* of course) at the homes of his milk route customers. I refused to accept any money from my father. I was just hoping to work off my guilt.

My parents let me end my appointments with Dr. Anolik after my first month back at VI. I convinced them I was doing well. I was going to school every day and my grades were excellent. I was going to stop seeing Dr. Anolik with or without their blessing. But I convinced my mother and father that Brother David and other teachers at VI served as better counselors for me than my psychiatrist.

I also believed my parents knew I was getting myself together.

Not that I didn't mess up. I did. Frequently. Certain events triggered intense feelings of insignificance, loneliness, and anger. And my trust issues were forever present like a scar I was afraid to look at. My occasional remedy for those incidents were morningless weekend nights intoxicated by the consumption of pint bottles of blackberry brandy and cans of cheap beer. But popping speed and acid became non-existent after my discharge.

Throughout the school year I often wondered what Brother David really thought of my weekly journal writing for his class. I was certain what I wrote had to jolt and taint his image of me being a typical high school student *getting myself back together.* I unloaded my life in my journals. Twice, when I returned to his classroom with his newspaper, he suggested we go outside to talk. We went across the street and sat on the graffiti covered bench at the *Down on the corner park.*

The park was home turf to my friends from Knapp's and Ridgefield. We were the dedicated teenage derelicts of Madison Avenue. The sight of me sitting with a member of a religious order didn't generate a more respectful behavior from the crew. And there was no hesitation with my friends to walk over and interrupt our conversation.

Sharon and Beth strolled over just to say, "Hey, Gregg."

Lemily stopped by and in his feigned gangster voice said, "Meet you in Knapp's when detention is over." And to Brother David he politely asked, "How's life, dude?"

And then Spaceman Ronnie visited, "What are you guys rapping about?"

"This is my teacher, Ronnie. Brother David." I hoped the formal religious title would be a message to Ronnie to back off. No luck.

"Glad to meet you, Dave. I fucking hate school. And I got three years left."

"Well...," Brother David replied, "School isn't for everyone. But I will pray for you. Pray that you find your way."

Ronnie laughed. "Ain't no prayer ever worked for me." He dribbled the basketball towards the hoop, took a shot, and missed badly. He turned and yelled back to us, "You'd think the fucking city would fix that broken backboard."

David and I talked about the weekend. I had crashed again. And my hangover and angrily charged thoughts filled the pages of my journal. The trigger: the first week of November. My child was born a year ago in November. So I was told. The father who didn't have a clue about anything throughout the pregnancy and birth. Nothing. Only the tidbits of news provided to me in the phone booth outside the A&P. And here I was back at VI during my one year anniversary of fatherhood which I wrote about in my journal.

On Saturday night at Ridgefield I chugged my pint bottles of blackberry brandy. Lemily and Eddie drank with me until the early morning. Mark was dishing out downers. I grabbed two. I got fucked up. The most fucked up since my hospital visit. So much for my resilience and coping skills.

I remember staggering home with Eddie and Lemily. Near St. Vincent de Paul's church, I screamed insulting drunken expressions at a passing car cruising over Partridge Street, "You fucking losers! Scumbags. Get lost. You fucking nobodies!" The hatred inside me exploded.

The car stopped. Four guys jumped out and beat the shit out of us. I was knocked out cold. Years later I remember meeting up with Mark and Lemily and talking about that incident. I asked them, "How did I get home? You never told me."

Lemily answered, "Your face got fucking stamped by those motherfuckers. So we put you in the mailbox and sent you home."

I wrote about that night and the beating in my journal. I wrote about my inability to handle my feelings as November approached. And I wrote that I didn't care anymore and that I just wanted to escape. I wrote that I felt alone and didn't want to deal with these feelings anymore. I ended my journal for Brother David with Nietcheze's quote, *And if you gaze long enough into an abyss, the abyss will gaze back into you.*

David listened. I talked mostly. Evening began to descend on the *Down on the corner park.* Eventually Brother David spoke.

"Gregg, you can't just make significant life events disappear. You can only put them on the back of the train in your life...and let them live there. You will cope much better whenever they surface. And they will surface. People aren't born resilient, Gregg. Resiliency evolves by handling the challenges in your life. The more challenges you handle, the more resilient you become."

"Yeah. Like I know when I'm not coping." I was ashamed of my weakness. "I know getting trashed is just a cop out. Everything is still so heavy. Far out, you know? And it still feels so close to me, like all that shit happened yesterday."

"But it didn't, Gregg. It didn't happen yesterday. You lost your child at an age when you were still just growing up. You have to deal with all that and stop beating yourself up."

My lack of a response caused Brother David to continue.

"More than a year has passed since the pregnancy and birth. And here you are. You got through. You survived. You put your life back together to the point where you will graduate and you're even thinking of college. You slipped on the ice and fell into what you like to say is your abyss. But you managed to climb back out. Now you have to alter your perspective on *your* life. Unless you want to quit on yourself. But I don't think you do, Gregg."

We finished our conversation and began to walk up Madison Avenue. David to the Brothers' residence, and me to Knapp's Tavern. As we were saying goodbye, David added, "Gregg, I know you are fond of Nietchse's words about the abyss, but I want you to focus on another quote from him, "To live is to suffer, to survive is to find some meaning in the suffering."

The only other time we had an extended after school conversation was in late March. Compared to the November session, the spring time conversation was mild. I decided to try out for the school baseball team. Vicious rumors about me flooded the school once I signed up for tryouts. I thought of quitting again. Not just giving up on trying to make the team, but quitting school again. I wondered if the ghosts of this past year would follow me for the rest of my life.

I tried to focus on Dr. Adair's final warnings while I was at E2 - *challenges in life will forever be part of your reality.* The comments I heard were cruel distortions of my past year. And the comments were embellished with hurtful lies and exaggerations.

I didn't want to quit school again. I didn't want to give up on myself again. When I told my father I signed up to try out for the baseball team, he twirled a forkful of dinner time spaghetti in front of his mouth as a smile of pride engulfed his face.

I didn't want to let my parents down...again. I was a good athlete. And a very good baseball player. But I never tried out for any school teams before this year, and I think I just wanted to prove to myself that I could make the team.

And I also wanted to play for my father. He loved baseball. He knew everything about the game. He was an admired and respected coach in the community leagues. And I wanted to see him watching me play again.

Some twenty years after my father died, I was at Graney's Pub on

New Scotland Avenue with the Albany Police Chief and some of his cohorts. Chief Tuffy was also a VI graduate. We were drinking pints and watching ball games on the large screen TVs. A Yankee player just stole second base with a hard slide and knocked the ball out of the opposing shortstop's glove. In a loud, and probably intoxicated voice, Chief Tuffy declared, "See that! Did you see that? He knocked the ball out of the glove," the Chief put his hand on my shoulder and shook me. "That would never happen on a team your father coached. He taught us how to *properly cheat;* to get an edge." The Chief took a swig of beer and continued with a demonstration for the other patrons in the pub. "This is how you tag someone out. You put the ball in your fist and close to the pocket of your glove. But the ball is never actually in the glove. It stays in your fist, inches away from the glove. And then you swipe at the runner like this..." As he performed his imaginary tag on an opposing player, he knocked three bottles of beer off the counter.

At the dinner table, my father brushed off the *prospect* of making the team. He knew I had the skills to be selected. He taught me from the day I was able to swing a bat and catch a ball. He knew I would make the team. And I was also certain I would be playing for the Vincentian Lions.

My father coached the Babe Ruth team I played on, the Albany Asphalt. When I was fifteen years old, in the last inning of the city championship game, I hit a long ball to the centerfield fence off the best pitcher in Albany, Nicky Farrell. I knocked in the winning run. Funny, whenever I think back to the "glory days" of that game, I don't remember my swing nor making contact with the ball. Nicky was a fast and intimidating pitcher. What I do remember is the Asphalt dugout erupting, and my teammates rushing towards me at second base to carry me off the field. I don't think there was ever a time my father was more happy for me.

The next year I played on the Troy Connie Mack team, which my father also coached. That season was the end of my formal baseball career. I couldn't focus on the game. I was constantly thinking of my child's pending birth...somewhere. I remember sneaking out of the dugout once because I was scheduled to make the long distance call at the designated time. I ran to the payphone by the concession stand with change jangling in my uniform pocket. I made the call.

I didn't get back to the dugout on time to go out onto the field for the next inning. My father substituted a player for me. On the ride home in the old station wagon, my father and I agreed I shouldn't finish the season. He knew from my mother what I was dealing with. So I left the team. And at the end of the season, my father left coaching.

Another cop out from the cruel memory bank of my life. And another scar in this teenager's bent existence.

Today, when I reflect on my youth, I am convinced I tried out for the VI team in hopes of erasing the hurt and embarrassment I caused my Dad in the Connie Mack League. I didn't care about some notch in my belt for making the team. I was looking to make amends with my father.

"Gregg, think about what you would be doing if you don't play for the Lions," Brother David contended. "If you quit on this, you are surrendering to the very demons you raged against the previous year. This is another step in taking your life back for yourself. Besides, you told your father you were trying out. Do you want to let him down?"

"No." I shrugged. I felt tense. I looked up at my teacher with a blank stare.

Brother David continued, "You often express in your journals feelings of insignificance. Being left out and feeling like you had no input or control over the outcomes in your life." He tapped my shoulder with his folded copy of the *NY Times*. "Don't let the students here, who are not even your true classmates, alter a decision you made for yourself."

The varsity team tryouts were at Bleecker Stadium. The negative comments from my current classmates were warming up as soon as I hit the field:

- "He's too much a druggie to make the team."
- "My parents don't think he should be allowed to try out."
- "He probably wants to get in with us just to sell drugs."
- "He's a fuckup. He won't even be able to see the ball. He'll be so stoned."
- "I'm surprised he didn't bring his low life druggie friends to the try-outs."

During a break we were allowed to walk across the street to the market. I walked behind everyone; quietly, alone, different. I kept my mouth shut until I heard one of my potential teammates say, "He won't be able to stay for the whole tryout. He's gonna have to go home and change a diaper." The group erupted into a boisterous laugh.

And that was it. I didn't go into the First Street market. I waited outside. When the *classmate* who made the comment walked out, I grabbed him and slammed him into the storefront. I locked his right arm behind his back and my other hand pressed into his throat. "You keep your mouth shut about me or I will make sure you can't open it again."

The Christian Lions quietly crossed the street back to the field. I went into the market and purchased a quart of Schaefer beer. I sipped from the paper bag as I chased down balls in centerfield. I am sure Coach Lynch thought I had a bottle of soda in the bag. But I didn't care. If I got kicked out of tryouts, at least I didn't get cut.

When I was called in to bat, I deposited the bag in the waste bin near third base. In all my years of playing baseball I never hit like this before. I made contact with every ball pitched near the strike zone.

I drilled balls throughout the field. I almost knocked out the pitcher with a fierce line drive up the middle. Coach Lynch was smiling and called out to the best pitcher on the team, “Davey, you pitch now. See if you can make Gregg swing and miss.”

But my bat connected with every pitch. My Louisville Slugger was like a powerful magnet.

I made the team. I was the starting center fielder for the Vincentian Lions.

Between baseball season and graduation, there were no other major events at the school except our Senior Prom. I didn’t attend. I didn’t have a girlfriend my senior year. But I kept Nurse Marie’s advice close to my heart. I kept *my heart open* and had several girls who remained *real* friends. I could have invited Sharon to the dance with me, but the thought of her putting on a formal dress, drunk and stoned, would have been too much of a struggle.

On the night of the dance, Kathy and I were drinking in the *Down on the corner park.* We watched the parade of my classmates being dropped off at the Madison Avenue entrance to the school. Slurring her words Kathy asked, “Why didn’t you ask me to go to the dance with you?”

“I don’t belong there, Kathy. Never fit in. And that’s not our scene. You know that. We’d have a shitty time.”

Kathy tried to stand but slowly crumbled onto the cement of the basketball court. “You could’ve at least fucking asked me, Gregg.” I lifted her into my arms and we sat on the park bench where she immediately passed out. Maybe we should have gone to the dance together. We would have been quite the sight.

Only a few weeks left until graduation.

CHAPTER SIXTEEN

June 1969 — The Prodigal Son Graduates

When all the dark clouds roll away
And the sun begins to shine
I see my freedom from across the way

— Van Morrison —

I did not attend graduation. No hard feelings. But from kindergarten through high school, until last year, my classmates graduated with the class of 1968. I never felt a connection with the class of 1969. I was fine with my teachers, but I was never welcomed or accepted by the students. I felt ostracized and disconnected during my senior year.

I told my parents I wouldn't be attending graduation. They understood. My ceremony, without the pomp and circumstance, was standing at the front window of Knapp's Tavern with some of the afternoon drinkers. We watched the Class of 1969 in their caps and gowns, march from the high school up Madison Avenue to St. Vincent de Paul's Church. We celebrated my graduation with shots of whiskey and glasses of Hedricks beer.

"They ain't your brothers, Man," Joey observed in a near stupor.

"Would have been fucking strange if you went." Lemily added.

"I can't picture you in one of those get ups." Noted Old Man Jitney. "That ain't you." And stuttering his words of wisdom Jitney added, "You belong here, Gregg. This is family."

After viewing the parade to the church, we went to a table and talked about our football game against North Albany on Sunday.

I was now a high school graduate but I felt nothing special. Did graduating mean anything to me? I didn't know.

An underage, but very excited Spaceman Ronnie rushed into the bar with the urgency of Paul Revere. He ducked to avoid the bartender and slouched over to our table, "That Brother guy I met, you know the dude in the park the other day? He asked me where you were...and he's coming here...with some other religious dude. The graduation ceremony ended and he is coming here to find you."

Spaceman Ronnie sat in the booth and Lemily poured him a beer from our pitcher.

Minutes later, looking completely out of place in their Brothers of Holy Cross attire, my two favorite teachers walked into Knapp's Tavern.

"We missed you tonight, Gregg," Brother David commented, standing at our table.

Old man Jitney negotiated, "Hey, you Brother people... if you promise to pray for me, you can have some of our beer."

"That's very nice of you, Sir." Brother Alfred answered. "But we're not staying. We just stopped by to give Gregg his diploma. But we will still keep you in our prayers."

Brother David handed me a large envelope. "You did it, Gregg. A little iffy back in September. But here is your high school diploma."

"Thanks." I was humbled. "I didn't expect to have my diploma delivered to me."

"Your name was called a few times at the ceremony." Brother Alfred handed me another envelope. "These awards are for you too, Gregg."

"Awards?" I looked at the manila envelope. "What's this?" I opened the envelope and avoided setting it on the table that was filled with empty shot glasses and spilt beer. I stared at the certificate. "Really. This is mine? And the awards too?"

"Four quarters and the final exam - all hundreds in Accounting," noted Brother Alfred. "The teachers had an easy time with the selection for the Business Award."

"Wow! You're the man, Gregor." Lemily took the certificates from my hand and examined the documents as if checking for their authenticity.

I continued, "I did not expect these Brother Alfred. Never had a clue this was coming down." My head nodded nonstop - not in disbelief but in a very strange, for me, sense of pride. I looked up at my business teacher, "I learned so much from you about accounting. You should get an award too, Brother Alfred. I never aced a course before in high school."

"We have one more award for you, Gregg." Brother David handed me the other envelope.

"Another one?" I started to open the sealed envelope.

"I have to confess, Gregg." Brother David said. "This one took me by surprise. The irony of you winning this award. In sports jargon someone may contend this award was fixed."

I tore through the sealed document and said with a stunned tone in my voice, "*The Effort and Achievement Award?*"

"Like I said, Gregg, maybe the fix was in. I mean *Achievement* I understand. But *Effort?*" My teachers shared a laugh. "You're here drinking at Knapp's and didn't even make the effort to attend your graduation."

"Oh my God. Wait until my parents find out."

"They know, Gregg." Brother David admitted. "Parents are notified after the selections are made. They knew you weren't attending."

"Now I feel like crap. I should have attended. For my parents."

"How the fuck do you feel like shit?" Old man Jitney asked, his words tumbling from his mouth in a mumbled slur. "Excuse my language, Mr. Brother." He took the certificates from Lemily. "You did good, man. You did real good, Gregor." His glassy bloodshot eyes examined each of the certificates. "And you know you ain't got no help from no one here."

I looked at my two teachers. I did feel like crap. "If I went to the ceremony, my parents would have seen me walk up to the altar three different times - my diploma, and then for each award. I can't believe I wasn't there with them. They would have lit up with pride."

Brother David put his hand on my shoulder, "But think about it...if you went to graduation, your father would have thought he had to put on a dress shirt and tie to attend. That's not your Dad's image. He would have been equally as uncomfortable in that outfit as you would have been sitting with the Class of 1969. I went to your house to break the news. Both your mother and father came to the door. Their faces glowed when I informed them of your awards."

"This is too fucking far out." A drunken Lemily stood from the table and announced. "School awards for the Kid. Baseball I can see. But school awards? We're gonna have another round of shots to celebrate."

"Not for me, young man." Brother David held up his hand to decline the offer. "I have to pack. I leave for Wyoming in the morning." My teacher worked at Ring Lake Ranch during summer. "We just wanted to stop by and give these certificates and award pins to Gregg." He turned towards me. "And you have my address for the ranch, right?" I nodded. "And you know I won't be back to VI next year so make sure you write."

"I will. I promise." I stood from the booth and thanked Brother David. Funny, so many decades later, I still don't think of him only as my English teacher. I think of Brother David as a teacher who helped me throughout the madness of my senior year in high school.

I thanked Brother Alfred. He shook my hand and congratulated me again, "I'll still be at VI next year, Gregg. So stop by any time."

And then my two teachers left the bar, departing from my own little graduation party with my friends at Knapp's Tavern.

Lemily nearly fell onto the table as he staggered back with three shots of Jack Daniels. He dropped himself into his seat and raised his shot glass with difficulty, "To Gregg, the high school graduate. And to all them fucking aces in accounting." We chugged the shots. "And to all those awards! *A's* across the board. Jesus fucking Christ! When we were in school together, I don't remember any of us getting any A's."

"That's not true, Lem. Remember that June years ago when we both got more A's than I did in Accounting. So many more. And on so many report cards. Both of us. Straight A students. I think we were in seventh grade. We went to the Glass House school building to help my father clean the classrooms. He had to finish early to make our Babe Ruth game. Remember?"

"Holy shit!! I do remember. That's fucking right, Gregg."

There was no stopping Lemily now from reveling in the glory days of our crime spree. "Yeah, man. We found Sister Constance's stash of blank report cards in her cabinet. Dig? Total blast at Hoffman's Playland." Lemily spoke directly to Old Man Jitney. "We grabbed a bunch of blank report cards. Free rides at Hoffman's for every A on *our* report card. So fucking far out. Gregg, remember how many times we rode the bumper cars for free?" Jitney and Lemily laughed. "But after a few days, Hoffman's was onto us. The manager and some security dude kicked us out. And they barred us from ever going again. What a head trip remembering that. Ain't never happened before we both got so many A's."

CHAPTER SEVENTEEN

Roadblock Challenges

If it wasn't for bad luck
I wouldn't have no luck at all

— Albert King —

As much as I love the blues song, "Born Under a Bad Sign," the lyrics do not relate to my life. The roadblocks for me the next few years were not because of "bad luck". I just fucked up and made stupid choices. Again.

I applied to St. Rose College right after graduation. The school was directly across the street from the technical building where my family lived. In 1969, the college became a coed school. Perfect timing for me. I also applied to SUNY at Albany. I applied to be admitted to their English programs.

I was rejected. Both schools sent me letters stating I would be accepted if I enrolled as a Business major.

Nothing like all those accounting A's and the Business Award backfiring on me.

Maybe St. Rose had another reason to reject me. A payback. A few years earlier, Lemily and I crashed a frat party at the then women's college. Eight "Rosebuds" threw a party in their dorm and managed to get two kegs of beer.

At the end of the night, the girls nervously tried to get rid of the kegs before there was the weekend dorm check. One keg wasn't even tapped.

Being the romantic, sensitive, knights in shining armor that we fancied ourselves, Lemily and I offered to take the kegs out of the dorms for the girls. Intoxicated, but out of an abundance of kindness in our hearts, we rolled the kegs across Madison Avenue and carried them into my bedroom behind the VI kindergarten class.

We didn't know how we would proceed with a story when my father found out, so we just told him the truth. We told him the whole frat party story and how the girls miscalculated how much beer they needed for their event. I emphasized to my Dad that Lemily and I felt sorry for the Rosebuds. And that we only wanted to help so the girls wouldn't get into trouble.

"That's the truth, Mr. Weinlein." Lemily chimed in to support our story. "The girls were so worried and so scared thinking they would get kicked out of school that they practically begged us to get rid of the kegs."

"Look, we even have the rental papers for the keg and the tap." I took the papers out of my back pocket and showed my father. "We said we would bring everything back to the beer store on time."

Shaking his head, wanting to believe but not certain, my father walked out of my bedroom. But my Dad was not a wasteful person. We put the keg in a large metal tub we found in the cellar, and for the next week we used ice from the milk truck to keep the beer cold. I think my Dad enjoyed being a regular presence in my room every evening to refill his pitcher.

And that's the story I tell to explain my rejection to St. Rose College. I suspect the school had some *big brother* camera that captured Lemily and I rolling the kegs across Madison Avenue.

My rejections to both SUNY Albany and the College of St. Rose arrived in the mail on the same day. For hours I cooled off by playing intensely physical games of hoop at the *Down on the corner park.* I didn't want to take business subjects. I didn't see myself as a business person. I knew I wanted to be an English teacher.

"Whaddya gonna do now about school?" Lemily asked, wiping sweat from his face with his t-shirt.

"I don't know. I really think I should go to college. I want to go." I was breathing heavily from the arduous game.

"I've been thinking." And when Lemily *thinks,* the outcome could be detrimental. He didn't go to college after his graduation in 1968. "I hear it's easy to pay for school with the student loans the colleges give you now. Why don't we get us some loans and go to the Junior College of Albany?" Lemily was a smart kid. Not classroom smart. Street-smart. But I questioned his self-discipline for college studies. I wasn't even certain I had the self-discipline for college.

"You'll go there?" I asked, thinking Lemily was joking. "To JCA?"

"Shit, Gregg...I'll try anything. You know that. If it don't cost me now. I'll try anything."

Neither of us had parents with incomes to make going to private college a viable option. I wanted to give college a try and I feared if I didn't attend in the fall, if I took another year off school, my formal education would have ended. "Okay Lem - If we can score the loans...let's do it."

We were approved for the student loans.

Hard to believe, but in September of 1969, Lemily and I were college students at JCA. Bring it on...

But our post-secondary educational careers didn't last long. Only until mid-October. We got our loans. But the loan money became the challenge that knocked me down again.

The process for securing a student loan along with the dissemination of funds is much more rigid today. In late August, before the fall semester began, we simply walked into the financial aid office at the Junior College of Albany and picked up our checks. And that was it... Hundreds and hundreds and hundreds of dollars in checks in our name.

Like I said, when Lemily gets *thinking,* it could be dangerous. We deposited the funds into savings accounts at the West End Bank on Madison Avenue across from Knapp's. A fiscally responsible initiative.

But we never made the final fall due date for our tuition payment.

Lemily was a gamer, a mastermind of scams created for instant gratification. "Gregg, we should fucking double this."

I should have known the long road to reap the benefits of a college degree did not fit his lifestyle.

We blew through our student loan money gambling at Kenny's Grocery on Second Avenue. His little store was his front to book bets. Initially we gambled only on NFL games, but once we got in the hole, we tried to dig out with NBA games.

The football games were a slow drain on our money because they were only on weekends. But once we started betting basketball, we gambled almost every day. We sat on the dilapidated stoop of a neighbor's porch next to Kenny's store. We listened to the basketball games on a transistor radio.

Seldom did we go back into the store to collect winnings.

We were withdrawn from our classes in mid-October for failing to pay our tuition. Our college career together ended with missed baskets by the team we bet on.

Another challenge and I fucked up.

Another year of my life wasted.

CHAPTER EIGHTEEN

Alas! An Associate's Degree

To define is to limit

— Oscar Wilde —

After my failed expedition into junior college, I soon realized my daily residency at Knapp's was getting old. For weeks the days of nothingness piled up, and so many of my friends had moved on. A few enlisted in the military, many had full time jobs, and some had partners and moved into adulthood with a family.

I needed a change. Desperately. I wanted to move beyond my troubled teen years. I wanted to grow up. Triggers and challenges still got the best of me sometimes. But I knew growing up would be the result of my choices and behaviors.

I picked up a part-time job at the Schulyer Pharmacy on Pearl Street, below Morton Avenue. And on days I didn't work there, I still helped my father out on his milk route. Working at the pharmacy was a step into adulthood. I learned about corruption, bureaucratic ineptitude, politics, and our government's inability to account for itself. At my job I learned that if a customer was paying cash, the cost of a prescription was much less than a customer using a medicaid card. I became a cynic of politics and game playing for profit in the business world.

At the pharmacy, I learned the drink of choice for many of my customers in the South End neighborhood was not the cheap alcohol like we favored at Ridgefield Park. Our best seller: bottles of Nyquil. No cold or flu symptoms required.

And I learned an ugly side of business working at Schuyler Pharmacy. One of my duties was to bring the canvas cash bag to the National Savings Bank seven blocks away at the corner of Pearl Street and Madison Avenue.

I was scared during those midday trips. Except for a few homeless winos slouched against vacant storefronts, I was the only white person on the streets. And I was still a teenager and small in stature. And except for a few interactions in baseball games, and my friend LeRoy at the hospital, I lived a disconnected life from minority populations. Yet there I was walking, maybe running, with a bag full of cash.

Decades later, I was back in the neighborhood of the Schuyler Pharmacy to drive my daughter to her volunteer position at the South End Children's Cafe. So many memories surfaced even though I worked at the pharmacy for only ten months. I took a leisurely drive around the streets. The pharmacy was no longer there. I drove up Pearl Street. The bank is now the African American Cultural Center. The car ride seemed short. But in memory, my trek with the cash bag was a journey that took forever.

On my ride home, I outlined a story in my head about my job at the Schuyler Pharmacy that became one of my annual Christmas pieces published in the Albany Times Union.

I also learned during my days at the pharmacy that I didn't want to spend my life in jobs like my gig there, or working four jobs like my father, just to support a family.

Luckily, my father knew a senior administrator at the junior college. He delivered milk to his home. The vice president. I met the dean a few times while working with my father. I'm sure it was another embarrassment for my mother and father when I blew my student loan money and had to withdraw from the college. But my parents were *always there for me* and once again…

The dean offered an arrangement to be readmitted to the college: take out a smaller student loan, pick the check up with my father, and sign it over immediately to my college tuition account. I also agreed to a work study program and have my earnings applied to my college bill. For two years I was a JCA library assistant. Sitting at the main door, I checked to see that the books being taken out of the library were properly stamped at the circulation desk and not being stolen.

My supervisor, Mr. Mendez, grew to appreciate my help and my sense of responsibility. I'm certain he wasn't aware of my past. And I wasn't going to tell him. I had a solid work ethic, and I was motivated by a sincere desire to make something of myself. Mr. Mendez often expanded my duties. Frequently I was asked to help out at the circulation desk and to assist students in the reference room.

On a few occasions, Mr. Mendez trusted me to close the library by myself at 9 pm. On those evenings, he always walked down the steps to the front door with me so he could demonstrate repeatedly how to lock the door.

One evening, March 3, 1972, we heard an alarming rattling and ominous rumbling in the sky. We saw a plane flying low above the Junior College of Albany campus. Very low. The noise from the engines was piercing, crunching, frightening. A short time later I heard a news bulletin on the car radio. Mohawk Airlines Flight 405 crashed into a residential neighborhood on Manning Boulevard, only a few miles from the library and just blocks from where I lived. Seventeen passengers were killed.

My favorite subjects at JCA were literature and history. And I was surprised at my enthusiasm for Spanish during my two years at the JCA. I excelled in those courses.

In May I graduated with an Associates Degree in Liberal Arts.

I did not attend my junior college graduation ceremony.

CHAPTER NINETEEN

Becoming a Teacher

The long and winding road

— Paul McCartney —

What a difference the massive recently constructed State University of New York at Albany campus was in comparison to the quaint New England like campus of JCA. I was thrilled when I received my university acceptance letter admitting me to the English Education program. The tuition was much less than the private junior college and I was able to handle the payments with my savings from work at the Schuyler Pharmacy along with money earned in the university work study program. Besides my acceptance, I was proud that I was going to SUNY Albany to become a teacher and I didn't have to ask my parents for any help.

My most difficult class was political science. My protestations and radical leanings as a teenager seem trite compared to those of the young adjunct instructor. She was a tall woman with short cropped hair who displayed a ferocious passion in her animated lectures. My grades were not cutting it. Professor Smith-Alou scheduled a meeting with me.

"Is there a reason you're not engaged in my class? You're a little older than the others. You lived through the sixties and our revolution. You're in college now so you didn't go to Vietnam, right? But you were here to fight the war at home. I would think you would be very interested in the topics covered in class."

The desk in my professor's office was cluttered with newspapers and magazines I never knew were published. And there were books stacked on a corner of her desk. Books by Abbie Hoffman, Gloria Steinem, Slyvia Plath, and Eldridge Cleaver. Her wall was decorated with anti-establishment posters and a large poster board with a message written with a black magic marker: *If you're not part of the solution, you're part of the problem.*

"Yeah. I know. Of course I'm interested in the topics." I responded shyly with only a hint of apology. "I just don't like to think about those years. Bad memories. My childhood friend, Kevin, was killed in Vietnam." I sat in a chair facing my professor. "He was only eighteen."

Leaning over her desk, my professor commented, "I would think that would make you more interested. Knowledge is power."

"I don't know...other friends of mine went too. A few made it back in one piece. But others came home only a fraction of what they used to be when we hung out. My friend MJ returned from the war and wore a necklace with the teeth from a dead VietCong soldier around his neck. So sick. It freaked me out every time I saw him. He was never the same when he got home."

Sympathetically, my instructor responded, "The boys who went were so young. Drafted into a war where we didn't belong."

"I mean - like I'm against the war. And I hated the politics that went along with the war. Maybe that's why I'm not engaged in your class. I try to detach from those memories...don't want to know, and don't care about politics, protests, or movements."

Professor Smith-Alou had piercing, tired blue eyes that penetrated the listener with her intensity. "That's not a roadmap to a passing grade."

"I'm supposed to graduate so I need to pass your class. All I have left is your class and student teaching. But things come up in your class and I flashback and I get angry - and then I just..." My professor stood staring at the political posters on her wall. I grew uncomfortable with the silence. And so I lied, "I mean I enjoy your class and I respect how much you believe in what you are teaching us."

She turned back to me. "Gregg, you have personal experiences that would be a huge contribution in class. But I think you are frightened by those experiences." My professor leaned over her desk closer towards me, "But sometimes it is the sharing of those experiences, the struggles, the victories, and the anti-establishment passion that builds a coalition and intensifies the movement. You understand?" She reached under a mess of folders for her gradebook and flicked through some pages to find my grades. "You're borderline right now." In a contemplative stance with her hand on her chin, she noted, "There is only a month left in the class."

Desperately, I interjected, "Sorry. I can focus more and do better."

"I don't want my class to be just about grades. But I do want your mind, your heart, and your soul to be into the subject matter." She tapped her pen against her chin. "Listen, I'm not going to flip my wig about this. Here's an alternative assessment for you. Let's do this. I still want you to come to class, digest what you can, find a way to make yourself more relaxed in class, contribute when you are up to it, do the papers, and take the quizzes." She closed the gradebook. "I want you to understand - this class is about our country and the way it is today. Our movement. And how we are fighting the war at home to make a better tomorrow. You need to improve your attendance in class. And you need to remember that *knowledge is power.*"

"I will. And I will try harder. And I'll do a good job with whatever assignment you give me."

I appreciated the meeting and the opportunity I was offered to pass Political Science and to graduate. I wish I could have told my professor what I really felt and how I thought all her "movement" crap was just that - bullshit to me. I wanted to tell her I did not believe wars would ever end. And I wanted to tell her I don't believe politics will ever truly be *for the people.* I even wanted to tell Professor Smith-Alou that I did not enjoy being in her class. Her presentations were so biased and manipulative. I felt like her students were being asked to conform to her beliefs like sheep; like characters in Ionesco's absurdist drama, "The Bald Soprano." We were to use our voice, yet be without *our* voice.

Still, I needed poly sci to graduate. I kept my mouth shut. In my head I could hear Simon and Garfunkel singing, "Silence is golden..."

My professor made her proposal. "Here's what you can do. In addition to the class final, you can submit a heartfelt portrayal of yourself during the war, your feelings about Vietnam, and your political beliefs. Between ten and fifteen pages. I will use that paper as an extra grade for your final average. Can you do that? The paper can be a combination of essay, short story, poem - that's up to you. If you do a good job with this, you will pass my class."

I am so glad I kept my mouth shut. I can do this. And I did. And I passed my political science class.

For years I had been jotting down images and thoughts about Kevin and MJ. I took on this assignment as a cathartic opportunity to frame those images and my emotions.

My paper included a poem I wrote for Kevin and MJ. A few years after my graduation from SUNY Albany, my poem was published in an anthology of Vietnam writings titled, *Demilitarized Zones:*

A Stripe

He made it back with a stripe and a scar
across his rough face. Before he left
we used to split a sixer of Bud and
each drink a quart of cheap river-water wine
every morningless weekend night.

He made it back with stories of war
and strange pleasures. He brought them
home from “over there.” He made it back
and with his thin shadow staggers
a cemetery of hate.

He made it back with a stripe and a scar
across his rough face. He still wears his field
jacket with his new blue Levis. He doesn’t
bother with cuffs or flares. He made it back
and his hair is just beginning to grow
over his ears. He made it back to our corner
and stands half alone and all confused
against the drug store window. He drinks another
Coke deep into this cold evening. Tonight seems
so peaceful and only cost
a “ten cent” bag of skag.

He made it back and was told he was honored for
doing his time. But I can't help thinking of
Kevin who doesn't wear Levis or split six-packs,
who doesn't drink wine and doesn't drink Coke
or shoot skag and never once had long hair.

He doesn't even hang around
on our corner any more.

And I can't help thinking of Kevin,
who still wears
his boots and uniform inside
the coffin that brought him home.

CHAPTER TWENTY

The Welfare Road to Student Teaching

When you ain't got nothing
You got nothing to lose

— Bob Dylan —

During my junior year at the university, I was in my first adult relationship with a woman who, ironically, attended the same private high school as my girlfriend when I was sixteen.

My graduation from SUNY Albany was on the horizon; only one semester to go.

Six years had passed since my hospitalization and the birth of my "secret" adopted child. And now, at age twenty-two, another child, a son, was about to come into my life.

I finished the first semester with decent grades. But with school and family responsibilities, I was only able to work part time. I received my student teaching assignment at the same time our family financial challenges mounted.

Fortunately, my older brother had climbed the career ladder working for the Department of Social Services. I had no clue what his job entailed or what social services even meant.

He phoned me to stop by his office and help with the softball lineup for the game that night. He also said he wanted to talk to me about my "situation".

Russ' desk looked like a hurricane blew through his window

overlooking downtown Pearl Street in Albany. Scorebooks, newspapers, softballs, team hats, uniform shirts, a pair of cleats, and a glove. Somewhere beneath the disorganization, I thought, there must be important documents related to his work. He was on the phone when I walked in. He put his hand over the receiver and whispered, "Go talk to PT. I'll be off in a minute."

I journeyed across the hall to PT's cubicle. He was the catcher on the team and looked very comfortable in his work space with his feet on his desk, head down, and his hands bracing his chin. "PT." He didn't answer. I raised my voice, "Hey, PT."

I woke him from his power nap.

PT told me my brother was in a panic because we were short a player for the game. Being socially polite, I asked PT about his job. The question threw him off.

Looking around his work area, PT appeared confused. Lost. He moved a metal coat rack. His softball uniform was neatly draped on a hanger. He derived his answer slowly and somewhat perplexed, he reached down and lifted a large poster onto his desk. "So this is our agency." He pointed to a spot on a complex organizational chart. "And we're here. This is our department. Right there. That's who we are." And that was as much of a job description as I was going to get from PT. I didn't mean for my question to be such a challenge or to be intrusive. I didn't mean to put PT on the spot or to make him feel uncomfortable.

My brother yelled from across the hall. "Gregg, I'm off the phone." I walked into Russ' office and could sense his anger. "Joey blew us off. We need a player. I called four possible players but no one can make the game." He picked up a piece of paper listing our batting order for the game. Joey's name was crossed off. "Anyone you know who we can call?" I didn't.

"Russ, your next interview is here," his secretary interrupted from the office entrance.

"Crap," my brother responded, "I forgot about the interview. Shit. He's here now?" His secretary nodded affirmatively. My brother pushed the softball gear and game materials onto the floor by his chair. "Sit over there, Gregg." He waved me towards an empty chair in the corner. "This won't take long. We have to get another player. Can you stay? We got to figure out the lineup for tonight. And I want to talk to you about your student teaching."

"I can stay."

"Send him in," Russ said to his secretary.

And to me, "This will be quick."

A tall man, dark hair, athletic build, in his mid twenties appeared wearing a light gray tailored suit. He shook Russ' hand, introduced himself, and handed my brother his resume."

Russ glanced through the resume. "Have a seat, Dan. So you went to Potsdam? Small world." The boss and the candidate sat down. "My wife is from the north country near Potsdam." They briefly discussed the job. My brother quickly outlined the job responsibilities.

In a very practiced and professional manner, Dan responded why he would be the right hire to handle those duties. "And I just got my place in Albany. So I'm ready to go if I'm hired. I think I would be a good fit in this agency."

The phone rang. Russ answered, "No. Not yet. I don't have anyone yet. I'll call you back later and let you know." I could tell from Dan's face he thought my brother was talking about the job still being open. But I knew better. My brother had priorities. We needed another player for the game tonight. Russ hung up the phone and sized up Dan asking, "This is unrelated to the position you're applying to and kind of off the record, but do you play softball?"

"I do." Dan responded hoping his answer was another unwritten bullet for his resume. "I played in a fast pitch league in Potsdam. I pitched and also played centerfield. But I can play any position."

"Can you make a game tonight?"

"Sure," responded the candidate applying for the job opening with the New York State Department of Social Services.

"OK. You're in." Russ reached down to retrieve his lineup sheet from the floor. He penciled in Dan's name. "Do you know where the circle is at the University? We play on that field. Six o'clock. We get there at about five thirty." He reached down to the floor again. "Here's your shirt and hat."

"And the job?" Dan also had priorities. "Is there a time frame before you make your choice?"

"You're in. The job is yours. I made up my mind. Shortstop tonight and a state worker tomorrow." My brother's mood changed immediately. Smiling, he said, "And, probably the most important thing is you're now officially on the Trollops softball team."

They stood and shook hands again. When Dan left, I moved to the chair by my brother's desk and wondered if my first interview for a teacher position would be like Dan's interview with my brother.

I mean...I play softball too.

"Jesus. That's a relief," Russ sighed. "What a coincidence. Now we're set for the game."

"Yeah. That interview worked out well." I moved onto the next topic. "You said you wanted to talk to me about student teaching."

"I do. I want to help you guys out. I have some connections working here. I remember you helped bail me out a few years ago. You were working at the Schuyler Pharmacy and I needed some money quickly to get out of a jam. You were saving up to get back into college. Remember?" I did remember. "And I was thinking...you're not going to be able to afford rent, groceries, and all the other expenses with the baby, plus school and student teaching."

"I worry about it all the time. I get so stressed out, you know? And after what happened when I was sixteen - I don't know - I guess

I wanted some type of normalcy in starting a family. But that seems like a stretch."

Russ opened a desk drawer and took out a sheet of paper. I saw my name on the top. "I had one of the girls type this out for you to bring home…all the benefits, addresses, where to apply, and contact information. Make sure you tell them you are my brother. You won't be able to stay in that apartment where you are now. Not at the rent you're paying. So give that landlord your notice and I'll get you into the new housing projects off Mount Hope Drive. The Ezra Prentice Apartments."

"Isn't that where Nana and Pa live?"

"Yeah. As soon as the projects opened I got them a place. And then more were built across the street. You've been inside. You know how nice the apartments are. Give your notice and get out of that apartment and then apply for social services. There will be a new unit across Pearl Street waiting for you."

"So...we would be on welfare?" There was a major stigma attached to being on welfare back in the seventies.

"Hey…it gets you through. I mean you are eligible with your income and family. You're not scamming the system or anything." My brother assured me. "And no one really has to know. You'll get a food stamp allowance and Medicaid for insurance. Once you're settled with Social Services, you just have to go there monthly for paperwork stating that your circumstances haven't changed. Bring this home." Russ handed me the printout. "Talk it over tonight. This will keep you above water. I just don't think you have another choice with your situation, Gregg. You know with student teaching, a baby, finishing college, and not being able to work. I'm sure you don't want to move back with Mom and Dad. Or with her parents?"

"Right. Those aren't good options. If I'm going to be a father - then I want to be a father." I smiled a nervous smile. Even if that meant with my brother's help.

"And you don't want to go the route you helped me with years ago?" I nodded. "Gregg, just look at this as something temporary. You'll graduate, have your teaching degree, get a job, and then you can put welfare behind you. But there is one obstacle. Her car. She has to get rid of the car."

"What do you mean?"

"You can't be on welfare and have a car. You're going to have to get used to riding the city buses and borrowing Pa Flynn's car."

"What? How do I do my student teaching without a car? SUNY could place me in another city. One of my classmates was assigned to a school twenty miles away."

"I worked that out too. I hope you don't mind. I already talked to Nana and Pa. They get to keep their car and live at Ezra Prentice as seniors with low income and no earning potential. You know, for medical appointments and everything. Their car sits in their parking spot all day. They told me you can have their car anytime. You know they're so proud of you becoming a teacher. And they're thrilled that you'll be living across the street from them. They get to see their grandson more."

CHAPTER TWENTY-ONE

Student Teacher Dilemma

Failure will never overtake me
if my determination to succeed
is strong enough.

My first student teacher assignment at a large suburban high school in Saratoga County did not work out. A week before my start date, I had my initial meeting with the principal and the English teacher whose classes I would teach.

English teacher: "I have two senior level college prep classes. The primary focus is the research paper. And I created my own curriculum for my three other classes. They were approved over the summer by the school board: *Science Fiction - The World Tomorrow*." The teacher handed me a syllabus along with paperbacks by Azimov and Bradbury, and a science fiction anthology. "You can start with a history of the genre and then assign whatever novel you are most familiar with to give yourself time to plan for the others."

Principal: "So you start next week, Gregg?" I nodded. "A week for lesson preparation and a week to get a haircut."

An awkward pause silenced the office.

"Anything else?"

English teacher: "I think we're set."

I stood. Uttered my perfunctory bullshit and thanked them for the opportunity. “Nice to meet you. I’m looking forward to being a part of your school.” And then to myself, “*Get me the fuck out of here!*”

I’m sure I put Pa Flynn’s old Ford to the test speeding down the Northway. A haircut? What the fuck was that about? The year I left high school I grew my hair down below my ears. Nothing extreme. No reason to have my hair cut shorter. And now this principal dropped a negative bias on me because of the length of my hair. Too fucking far out. And three science fiction classes. I never read science fiction before and I never had a high school or college assignment related to science fiction.

I drove straight back to the university hoping to catch my student teacher supervisor. A middle-aged man who always wore a suit and spoke in elongated sentences packed with educational jargon. His voice intimidated most of the students in his Teaching Methods class and he projected the image of an intellectual. Mr. Ricter was conservative, task oriented, and demanding. There was no gray area in class. He followed his lesson plan: *you do this to get that* was his requirement to pass. But I always thought his authoritarian projection was his effort to model for us the importance of being an authority figure in our classrooms. A favorite phrase of his was often injected into his lectures with: *your classroom, your responsibility.*

Near the Education Building I saw my student teacher supervisor walking near the campus fountains. I ran to catch up to him.

“Mr. Ricter...do you have a minute?”

“Good morning, Gregg. Did you survive your meeting with your cooperating teacher and the principal this morning?”

“No. I think I’m done at that school before I even start. I came right back to campus because I need to talk with you.”

“Then we need to chat. Let’s go to the campus center.” I struggled to keep up with his long strides. “What a glorious break in the weather. And such a joy seeing everyone outside, walking on campus instead of using the tunnels to get from building to building… and seeing the students hanging out by the fountains. I will enjoy this image of an early spring. Winter has been too long." He waved dramatically towards the mass of students congregating near the large marble structures.

The campus center was a continuous explosion of noise from seventies rock music and the boisterous chatter of voices. And of course, from the balcony, the daily political rants from student protestors with intentions of changing the world.

We got coffee and found two chairs in a much quieter area in a room on the second floor. "I'm not going to make it at the school where I'm placed, Mr. Ricter."

"What's the problem, Gregg?" Once our placements began we only saw Mr. Ricter on days he visited our assigned schools to observe our class. But I had him measured. I saw through his *act.* The hard-ass instructor was an unexpectedly cool cat who was caring and kind. He preferred that his students did not know about his more compassionate side. The sensitive image would be incongruent to the one Mr. Ricter liked to project in the classroom.

"This morning was a disaster." I answered.

"Was there an issue at your meeting?"

"More than just an issue." I stirred my coffee. "I mean like I knew right away it wasn't going to work there. The cooperating teacher assigned me three of his science fiction classes. Science fiction! I'm not down with that. When he handed me his syllabus…I mean I knew some of the authors by name but I never had any interest in that genre. I think it's crazy. I took as many literature classes as I could here but never had a science fiction class. And like you said in class, Mr. Ricter, you need to 'have passion for what you're teaching'. Hard to have a passion for something you don't have a clue about."

With a facetious smile and an unorthodox attempt at linguistic humor, Mr. Ricter noted, "So science fiction ain't your passion?"

I couldn't even fake a smile. "I mean it's stupid getting assigned those classes. I need to graduate." I tend to ramble on when I am upset and I nervously spilt some coffee on my jeans. "Do they even have science fiction courses here? I might as well have been assigned to teach Math somewhere. Like I struggle just to get through each day. I don't give a crap about some future world."

I handed Mr. Ricter the syllabus for the science fiction classes. His head swayed from one side to the other as he reviewed the document. "You have a point, Gregg. We need to do a better job at placement and matching up student teachers with cooperating teachers. Maybe the School of Education needs to ask cooperating teachers who want to work with our student teachers to submit their syllabus before we place our students."

"I'm not looking for any favors, Mr. Ricter." (Although I was.) "But you know my situation. I have transportation issues and I got placed in a school twenty-five miles away from my apartment in the projects. I have to borrow my grandfather's car to get to student teaching. I'm kind of freaking out about this." I carefully took another sip of cafeteria coffee. "This is a real bummer. I just wanted this to work out, two months left…you know…to go smoothly and graduate."

"And how is the baby, Gregg? You have a student teaching problem but always keep in mind what is most important in your life now."

"I know. I know. But getting my degree and teaching *is* about my family. It would be the life I want to have for the family. You know, to get a teaching job in September and get the hell out of the projects."

"Unfortunately, I'm not really involved in the student teacher placements. The education secretary has that responsibility. They get a list of schools accepting student teachers and they go from there. But there has to be a more understanding system. Especially for our students with unique situations. Let me see what I can do."

CHAPTER TWENTY-TWO

Schalmont High School Student Teacher

I'm starting to see the bigger picture
I'm beginning to color it in

— Mike Scott —

Mr. Ricter called my home in the evening, "Hello, Gregg…there are very few options left since most schools have already filled their student teacher requests. Schalmont High School has an open spot. And I personally know your supervising teacher. Schalmont would be a good fit for you. The main problem is the school is a good distance from the university and even longer from where you live. But there are three other UAlbany students going to Schalmont."

"If I can work out a carpool with them that will be great. I'd feel guilty asking my grandparents for their car every weekday. Thanks, Mr. Ricter."

"I think you will be able to carpool. Call Schalmont tomorrow and leave a message for Mr. Sisario to set up an introductory meeting. One more thing, Gregg…" I could hear soft smirking laughter coming from the other end of the line. "I found out there are a couple of hippies on the staff there with long hair, and Pete Sisario doesn't teach any science fiction classes."

"This is such a relief. Thanks again, Mr. Ricter."

"Now just do the job you're capable of doing and take care of the classes. And, most importantly, find a balance with student teaching and your family. I will see you at Schalmont when I stop by to observe. And don't hesitate to call if there are any issues."

Like I said before...a real hard-ass, Mr. Ricter.

At our final Methods class meeting, Mr. Ricter helped organize carpools for students placed outside the Albany area. "There are many benefits to carpooling," he told the class. "In addition to conserving energy, reducing pollution, and limiting the amount of gas money you will need, the greatest benefit is the education that will take place with the students you are riding with each day. You will learn from each other. Learn what other teachers are like and find out their expectations for their student teachers. You will learn about different types of students and get a sense of family issues that can cause a student to tank. And you will learn how and why students behave differently in different classes. You will learn the *reality* of school discipline policies. Motivational techniques. Classroom management strategies. The relationship between teachers and administration. You will learn that some schools are *the haves,* and other schools are *the have nots.* The ride to your school should be like a team meeting. And your ride back after school is your opportunity to decompress and vent. So if your mode of transportation is carpooling, and for most of you it is, engage with your fellow student teachers."

Schalmont High School proved *the perfect fit for me.* Not nearly as large as the school where I was first placed and not as small as the Vincentian Schools I attended. My student teaching experience at Schalmont was remarkably positive and helped me grow to become the teacher I always wanted to be.

I carpooled to Schalmont with the three other students. Our conversations made the ride seem shorter. But there were no real connections made. I don't remember the name of a single student in the carpool. All I remember is that each of them called Long Island home.

Transportation to Schalmont was long, tedious, and always a challenge. The distance from my apartment at the Ezra Prentice housing projects to SUNY Albany was over five miles. Schalmont High School was another twenty miles from campus. My carpool companions lived at the university.

On days I drove, I picked up Pa Flynn's car and made the long trek over Pearl Street and up Western Avenue to collect my carpool mates.

Transportation distance from the projects to Schalmont: 25 miles
Transportation time when I drove: 45 minutes

On the days I rode with the other Schalmont student teachers, I felt my transportation itinerary was almost as long as my time in the classroom. I became very familiar with the city and UAlbany bus systems.

The sun was just beginning to rise when I left the Ezra Prentice Projects to board the earliest bus at the corner of Mt. Hope Drive and South Pearl Street. I asked for a transfer ticket and changed to the Western Avenue bus at State and Pearl Street. I rode that bus out of downtown Albany and up through the Pine Hills neighborhood where I grew up. At Manning Blvd, I exited the city bus and waited for the green SUNY bus.

Transportation distance to Schalmont: 25 miles
Transportation time including bus trips: 85 minutes

On the days when I took the buses, I left my family before sunrise and returned home in the evening.

Mr. Sisario, my cooperating teacher, will never be forgotten. Not so much for his knowledge of subject matter, or his insights in instructional methods, but for his willingness to believe in me and to trust me.

After a specific number of school days, the cooperating teachers turned the classes over to their student teachers. I recall from my carpool conversations that the student teachers took over instruction for the final two weeks. My experience was much different.

Mr. Sisario informed me he was having surgery three weeks after I started student teaching. He said he wouldn't be back to school until a few days before my time at Schalmont ended.

"I discussed this with our principal, Gregg, and with your supervisor." Mr Sisario sat in his teacher chair wearing a wrinkled white shirt and a blue tie loosened around his neck. "I would like you to take over my classes while I'm out. I know student teachers mostly observe and then take on the classes incrementally, but I've watched you interact with my students and I have seen you take a lead instructional role in the classroom. My surgery is going to keep me out for a few weeks. How would you feel if I didn't get a substitute and you taught my classes? Schalmont is like other schools, we're hit or miss with substitutes. My students would be much better off with consistency and a teacher they already know and respect."

I tried to mentally digest what I was being asked. "You mean I would be teaching your classes by myself all the days that you are out?"

"Gregg, I know you have only been here a short time but I know you can do the job. You have a good grasp of subject matter. You do a great job preparing. My students are engaged and want to work for you. They like you and they want to learn from you."

My confidence skyrocketed because of Mr. Sisario's comments. The challenge of his proposition appealed to me. "You wouldn't have to get a substitute teacher?"

"That was my conversation with the higher ups and with the other English teachers. Sometimes it is difficult to get a substitute to commit to weeks of covering a class. Most substitutes want the freedom to be where they want to be on the days they want to substitute. The amount of time I will be out could be a long stretch for a substitute teacher. I have the go ahead on my end. The English department also thinks the students would be better off with you, someone they know, instead of a substitute. What do you think? You can take some time to think it over."

"Wow. Like..." (I caught myself saying those two words out of habit and promised myself I would stop.) "And you think I could handle this by myself, Mr. Sisario?"

"I do. We all do. Besides, in terms of support, you wouldn't really be by yourself. Each of the English teachers has promised they will take care of you while I'm out. Gregg, do you remember last week in the creative writing class, when you read the poem you just published in the university newspaper?" I nodded. "You went through your whole writing process: the incident, the why and how you came to write the poem, the emotional effects you hoped your poem would generate in readers. And you even talked about the publishing process. That was an invaluable lesson. You are far beyond me as a creative writing teacher. When we do creative writing, I'm more like a coach in a sport I never played before. But not you. So I am very confident if you take my classes. What do you think?"

What do I think? I wasn't thinking. I was feeling. Feelings that have been a long time coming for me; feelings of self-worth waiting to erupt from inside. I was feeling pride, acceptance, confidence, and appreciation. I was feeling there was *purpose and responsibility* in my life in addition to my family. I was feeling great.

"I would like this... as a personal challenge and a chance to prove something myself. I don't know how to thank you for trusting me like this. And for believing in me."

"Gregg, I am the one to be thanking you."

And as the semester progressed, I was fine with my extended time of primary instructional responsibilities. But there was so much prep work. I quickly learned being prepared made the school day go more smoothly.

My final take away from my student teaching experience: I definitely wanted a career as a high school teacher. I was proud of myself for making a career choice I was passionate about. I also gained a sense of confidence working with teenagers along with a sensitivity for students who brought their life challenges into the classroom.

Been there / Taught that. Teaching made me feel my world was complete. My resurrection from the debris of my teenage years was solidified.

In May I graduated from SUNY Albany with my BS in Secondary English Education. My diploma arrived by mail in June. I did not attend my college graduation ceremony either. No celebration. No tossing a cap in the air. With the little money I had, instead of the rental fee for a cap and gown, I took my family to the Orchard Tavern for pizza and we celebrated together.

A month later, I received my teaching certificate from the New York State Department of Education.

For the first time in my life I felt my vision was clear and with meaningful purpose:

Get a teaching job.

Get off welfare.

Provide for my family.

CHAPTER TWENTY-THREE

A Teaching Career Begins

We've been through...
Self hurt
Plastics, collections
Self help, self pain,
EST, psychics, fuck all

— Michael Stipe —

Been there / Taught that has been my journey to move beyond a very challenging adolescence where I wallowed in the quicksand of rebellion, rejection, and self-destructive decisions.

Final cost of my poor decisions = two years behind most of my classmates who sailed through high school and then onto college or work opportunities.

Two years behind.

I lost my first year because I dropped out of high school.

And I lost a second year when I withdrew from college to pay off gambling debts with my student loan.

My initial thought when I reflect on those lost years: "What an asshole!"

But as I worked through this memoir, I realized the inspirational sense of self-worth and resilience that comes with putting broken pieces of a life back together. My rebound and my reward in life culminated with a purposeful and rewarding thirty-five year teaching career.

Not all aspects of my adult years were a blessing filled with success. But my adult mistakes and failures seemed easier to overcome once I began to believe in myself. I confronted those shortcomings. I didn't try to escape.

Throughout my career, and the latter years of my life, I kept close to my heart the scarred memories of my teenage years; the abyss of drug and alcohol abuse, teenage pregnancy, suicidal ideation, and ill thought decisions. And never did I forget my week in a psychiatric hospital.

I was a dangerously at-risk teenager who became a teacher of troubled students.

CHAPTER TWENTY-FOUR

My First Interview

I don't give a damn for the same
old played-out scenes
I don't give a damn
for just the in-betweens

— Bruce Springsteen —

I followed the directions from the switchboard operator to the Campbell Van Norton School. Turning left off Route 22, I drove past a large entrance sign with the words, *Berkshire Farm Center and Services for Youth.*

Canaan, New York was near the western border of Massachusetts. I had never been there. I only knew the name of the school where I was being interviewed.

I parked the car in the faculty lot.

"Excuse me?" I asked a man sweeping the sidewalk near the school. "I have an interview with Mr. Martins but I'm thirty minutes early. The drive was much quicker than I thought. Is there anywhere I can drive to for a coffee?"

"An interview with Percy?" He leaned against his broom smiling. "You can call him Mr. Martins today if you want. But if you get the job you call him Percy like everyone else here. I'm Nick. One of the groundskeepers at The Farm."

"I'm Gregg." We shook hands. "Nice to meet you, Nick."

"Likewise. You said you're thirty minutes early, looking to kill some time. Then I'd suggest you take a hike up to one of the cottages and see where the boys live." His hand waved in a circular motion encompassing the different dorms on the campus. "Nevermind. This is lunch hour. Boys will be in the cafeteria. You know..." Nick thought. "Better yet...take a drive down to the private beach on the lake."

"Private beach? What lake?"

"Queechy Lake, man. The Farm has a beach on Queechy Lake. The staff take the boys there during rec time after school and on weekends when the weather's right. And some teachers go there for their lunch period. You should check it out. One of the perks working here."

"I'll do that. Thanks for the tip, Nick."

Back in my car, I drove past an area of farmland with an abundance of crops which I learned were harvested and utilized for meals on campus. Turning onto a dirt road, I found the beach and parked my car. I sat at a picnic table and prepared for my interview staring at the tranquil waters of Queechy Lake.

"This is a beautiful campus, Mr. Martins," I said after being escorted into the assistant principal's office. "Didn't expect to have an interview at a school with a private beach on a lake." Mr. Ricter taught us to converse in a factual but casual manner; to make yourself as interesting a person as a prospective teacher. Not to be long winded in responses to questions. And to conclude the interview with a conversation beyond the job *to break the ice* of formality.

The assistant principal was a tall thin man wearing large black glasses. His striped tie was loosened over his white button down collared shirt. "So you got to see some of Berkshire Farm?"

"Yes. I was here a little early. I met Nick and he suggested I take a drive to the lake. The grounds are beautiful here."

"Nick's a good man," Percy said. "The campus dichotomy is that the physical beauty of The Farm is offset by the challenging and unpredictable behaviors of our students. We have a population of very troubled teens who are sent here by the juvenile courts. PINS. Persons in need of supervision." Percy unwrapped a piece of gum. "Currently there are over a hundred students living in our cottages and going to school. Besides our educational component, the students get mental and emotional support here. We have staff twenty-four-seven at each cottage. And each cottage has its own social worker and cottage coordinator. The boys also receive counseling with our psychiatrist, Dr. Bell."

A pause in the assistant principal's presentation warranted a question, "So the students committed a crime to be sent here?"

Mr. Martins nodded. "Sort of. The boys are sent to us from all over New York State through family courts and are placed on PINS for an assortment of offenses like truancy, robbery, drugs, or violations of probation. We get funding from departments of social services. Placements seem to be cyclical. Some years more boys are sent from the boroughs of New York City. Some years from Buffalo. Recently, a large number of boys have been sent from Rochester and Syracuse."

"How long do the students stay here?" I was interested. I learned of this job at the UAlbany Placement Office, but there were no details about the facility. The job listing was simply a teacher vacancy notice. I only knew that Canaan, New York was a fifty minute ride from Albany.

"Usually less than a year." Percy continued. "But that is up to the courts, their probation officers, and a review of evaluations we do here." The vice principal continued to tell me how the school was just one component of the Berkshire Farm Center and Services for Youth. Eventually, we talked about the English opening. Holding my resume and application in his hand he asked, "So you graduated from SUNY Albany. There are other staff members who went to college there. Why do you think you would be a good fit for a teaching position here?"

After my conversation with Percy, he took me to the main office and introduced me to the school principal, Mrs. Ester Boughton. We talked briefly.

Back in the parking lot I thanked Percy for the interview and shook his hand.

"I am glad to have had the chance to meet you. Mrs. Boughton and I will have our discussion after the final interview this afternoon. We'll go through the applications again of our finalists who were interviewed. And then I'm sure we will be offering the job to someone by the end of the week."

"I appreciate the opportunity to see the facility and to learn about the different programs offered to the students." I looked beyond the school and noticed how the Berkshire Mountains provided a picturesque backdrop to the campus.

"Last question..." Mr. Martins took off his glasses and replaced them with a dark pair of sunglasses. "You do know you would be teaching in a classroom composed of very difficult male teenagers, and that would be no problem for you? And you would be comfortable in this educational setting at Berkshire Farm?"

For a second I thought of telling Mr. Martins that I lived on similar turf as a teenager and that I was surprised I was never sent here. But I rejected that thought. "I hope I get the call, Mr. Martins. And yes. I would be very comfortable teaching here."

CHAPTER TWENTY-FIVE

My First Teacher Position

A broom is drearily sweeping
Up the broken pieces of yesterday's life

— Jimi Hendrix —

I didn't have to wait until the end of the week to find out the status of my application to teach at Berkshire Farm. My phone rang that same evening. Mrs. Boughton called and offered the job to me.

Esther Boughton said the summer school session ended in late August and there would be a "home leave" break for the students before the start of the new school year. She encouraged me to stop by during that time to get acquainted with the school and teachers before I officially started in September.

I had my first teaching job.

Six years after my breakdown and my week in a psychiatric ward, I had my high school diploma, a college degree in education, and now a teaching position. If I hadn't put up my own roadblocks, maybe I would have begun my career two years earlier. But September 1974 was fine with me. Time to loosen the chains of my guilt complex.

And like Jimi sang, I did "sweep up the broken pieces of yesterday's life."

No one on campus called the Campbell Van Norton School by its name. To the staff and students, we were all part of "BIF" or "The Farm". I also learned from Tom the Music Teacher whose daily attire was sandals, a polo shirt, and shorts, that I shouldn't bother with a shirt and tie. He advised jokingly, "They'll choke you with your tie when you break up a fight."

I became friends with Peter the Duty Officer who was stationed in a key position in the main hallway. He kept his walkie talkie in his hand at all times. Pete was first in the classroom whenever a student outburst erupted. My classes at The Farm were not going to be like my student teaching days at Schalmont High School.

Academic memories of my seven years at Berkshire Farm elude me. I do recall our educational reports for each student: subject, grade, reading level, and comment six times during the twelve month school year. The focus at Berkshire Farm was *the whole student,* which Doctor Bell emphasized at our staff meetings. Classroom success was only a part of the "milieu therapy" at The Farm.

The majority of my students were seriously remedial. A few of my tenth grade students read below the third grade level. But their academic gains during the year were significant.

Why was school success here, with a student population of educationally challenged and socially disadvantaged teenagers, so dramatic?

Seven years later when I started teaching at a public school, I figured out the reasons. Granted my conclusions are anecdotal and unscientific, but I am convinced they are worthy of consideration:

1. *Students attended school.* At Berkshire Farm, my students were escorted to school daily by their cottage staff. Absenteeism occurred only when a student's illness was confirmed by the campus nurse or if a student had run away and was AWOL. But the threat of a student's placement at Berkshire Farm being extended because of an AWOL, or the threat of being moved to a more secure detention center, were both effective deterrents. And even more note-

worthy, students at Berkshire Farm were in school all year. Summer session was mandatory.

2. *Academic support was extensive.* Each student was scheduled into remedial Math and Reading. And academic support was extended beyond the school day. Homework was a requirement and assignments were completed with staff assistance in the evening at the cottages. I learned the extent of this strict support during my first week at Berkshire Farm. I began class with a very perfunctory teacher question, "Did you do your homework?" Johnny from the Bronx answered assertively, "We ain't got no fucking choice here, Teach."

3. *Mental and emotional support was constant and consistent.* Each cottage had its own Social Worker working with students. Dr. Bell was on campus. A medical team worked at the campus infirmary. And, if you were not a supportive adult, whether at school or at the cottage, you didn't work for long at Berkshire Farm.

4. *A positive and life affirming environment was always present.* I learned quickly just how much this mattered to the students at The Farm. One of my students was discharged early for good behavior and academic progress. He had already been at Berkshire Farm for five months before I started teaching. The staff said I wouldn't recognize Earl if I knew him when he arrived on campus. He was angry. Non-compliant. Explosive. Threatening. But the Earl in my classroom the past two months was respectful, helpful, and hopeful. Five weeks after Earl's discharge he was driven back onto campus by the state police. Let an at-risk delinquent adolescent live and grow in a positive and supportive environment,

and life-affirming changes will be numerous. Put that same rehabilitated student back into a negative environment surrounded by drugs and alcohol and violence, and the gains will disappear quickly.

For certain all I learned at Berkshire Farm inspired me throughout my educational career. Berkshire Farm did not provide me with memories of noteworthy academic success stories. But the memories I carried into my retirement were of at-risk students putting the pieces of their lives back together - even if only for their time at Berkshire Farm Center and Services for Youth. Those memories enhanced my approach in the classroom. Embedded in my mind throughout my career was a lesson I never learned at the university: *there will be days when academics have to be secondary.*

This belief gave me a foundation enabling me to have a rewarding career teaching at-risk youth.

CHAPTER TWENTY-SIX

George From Buffalo

But if dreams came true
wouldn't that be nice

— Bruce Springsteen —

Big George is a cherished memory of my days at Berkshire Farm. His head tilted forward to walk though my classroom doorway. He was only fifteen, still growing, and already six-five.

"Mind your head, George," I reminded him, referencing a favorite Irish expression. At the faculty basketball games during our extended lunch periods, we all predicted George would be playing in the NBA someday.

But George had more immediate plans for future earnings, and sports were not his thing. He never thought about further down the road in life. Instant gratification only for Big George. His optimistic financial plan was set to kick in as soon as he was discharged from Berkshire Farm.

Unlike Big George, most of the youth at Berkshire Farm struggled to be positive about their future. Despite the enhanced self-worth our students felt while at The Farm, the majority sensed ever present barricades to their dreams once back home.

Still, the staff listened and encouraged our students.

Jamal was going to sing with the Commodores. He danced his way down the halls singing, "Brick House."

Jon-Jon played on the school basketball team and fancied himself being signed by the Knicks.

Rico could argue with anyone, especially with the staff. And he had the spunk and intellectual capacity to do so. A lawyer, right? No chance. Rico was going the distance. "I'm gonna be one of those dudes in the black robes just like the one who sent me here."

And Dewayne was so cool and so slick. The boys in his cottage nicknamed him *Cruise.* He complained daily that the Farm was not co-ed. Can you imagine? And Dewayne's future plan? When he was discharged he was going to hook up with Pam Grier. "She's so foxy, Mr. Weinlein."

And what was Big George's future plan? His plan had a criminal element that would likely impede his success. Still, Big George was determined. Adamant. Focused. His plan was clever but also preposterous. The staff concluded our student created his tall tale to "bust" on us.

Big George told us in vivid detail how he was going to pull off his big score. His plan was to go to the hospital back home in Buffalo posing as a newspaper boy selling papers. He would then enter the rooms of patients who were out for appointments and steal their money and jewelry.

The staff could not shake the humorous image of our six foot-five fifteen year old posing as a newspaper boy at the hospital.

"George...," I said, congratulating him and saying goodbye on his discharge date, "listen to your English teacher one last time. Reconsider that plan of yours for when you get back home. You know you could just get a job as a newspaper boy."

"No way, Mr. W. That'd just be change and singles. I need to grab some big-time bucks. I'll come back and visit you in my new Caddy."

George's freedom lasted only a week. Midway into my class, the Duty Officer escorted him back into my room. "George missed your class, Gregg. He's back already."

"George. Long time no see." I greeted him near the doorway. "What happened?"

Sullenly, George looked down at me. I think he even grew during the week he was gone. "I guess I made one mistake, Mr. W. Threw my whole plan off and got me caught."

"What went wrong, George?"

With boyish innocence, he detailed his miscalculation which led to his arrest. "I think I should have just grabbed some newspapers at a store. But I stole a newspaper truck instead." George was upset with himself. "And parked it in front of the hospital."

CHAPTER TWENTY-SEVEN

Hooping It Up at Lunch Time

Basketball jones
I got a basketball jones

— Cheech & Chong —

One of the employee benefits of working at The Farm was the ninety minute lunch break in the middle of the school day. During lunch period, the boys were taken back to their cottage to wait for their scheduled time to be escorted to the cafeteria. A few cottages at a time.

The school staff had several options at lunch. Most teachers ate in the cafeteria, then returned to the faculty room for conversation and newspaper reading. Others went back to the classroom to work on lessons, and the few teachers who lived in the Canaan area went home for lunch.

Mental health experiences were also a popular lunch time break; a slow cruise around Queechy lake or a short drive to the quaint town of West Stockbridge.

And then there were teachers locked into the *Basketball Jones* syndrome. The fanatics of glory days that never happened nor ever would. But there we were on the court during lunch period *jonesing* for basketball stardom in a delinquent school gym.

Six teachers played basketball for an hour every school day. Mark and Brian, social workers and cottage coordinators, sometimes played in the games.

Mannerisms on the court mimicked favorite players. Mostly hoop stars from the Knicks. Roger the Artist was in constant motion with a rhythmic outside shot just like Bill Bradley. The only difference being Roger the Artist's shooting percentage was well below Bradley's.

Big Bill was our Willis Reed. Four or five inches taller than the other players. He controlled the boards and shot mostly two or three feet from the basket.

Eddie was like DeBusschere - intense, physical, and moving players out of his way when he went to the hoop.

Chuckie thought of himself as Earl "The Pearl" Monroe. The key phrase being *thought of himself.* He dribbled every which way...but went nowhere. Unlike Earl, all Chuckie's moves had no purpose and were often comical. He passed the ball from behind his back and even between his legs, always missing his teammate.

I fancied myself as Walt "Clyde" Frazier, playing with contained intensity and an obsessive desire to win. I'm certain my obsession had something to do with my size. I was always the shortest player on the court. But the one thing missing in my impersonation of Clyde was my teacher attire. It definitely lacked the wild fashions of Clyde's expensive wardrobe.

The only hoopster without the nickname of a Knicks player was Wickzy the music teacher. He was the least skilled player on the court. And always the last to arrive. While most players rushed out of our classrooms to the gym, Wickzy ran out to his car and devoured a box of donuts for his pregame ritual.

The hoopsters felt obligated to come up with a nickname for Wickzy. After our games, we took a dip in the Olympic size pool adjacent to the courts. Roger the Artist commented, "Wickzy, you were awesome today. Just like Julius Erving. Two baskets! After the way you played, from now on we're going to call you, 'Dr. D.' after

Dr. J. The 'D' is for your donut ritual. Dr. D." Wickzy's new nickname caused an eruption of laughter in the pool.

After a quick swim in the pool and then a proper shower, we packed away our basketball attire, dressed in our teacher outfits, and rushed back to our classrooms.

Percy Martins failed to mention the unique employment benefit of a noon time basketball league that came with a teaching job at Berkshire Farm. If you chose to be part of the lunch time hoop crew, you ended up in the best shape of your life. Unless you ate a box of donuts or a cake before the games.

The most physical games occurred when the cottage staff showed up to play against the teachers. Those games were often marred by intentional fouls and an abundance of shoving. But there were no real fights or loss of friendships. Win or lose, we managed to remember we were just playing a game. More importantly, we were able to make real connections with staff members from other agencies at The Farm.

Those connections we made on the basketball court often carried over into our work with the boys. We became a unified team of employees long before "staff development" became an educational buzzword.

Not that I am saying staff development was more real and beneficial on the basketball court.

Actually, being honest, that is exactly what I am saying.

CHAPTER TWENTY-EIGHT

Science Exam Substitute Teacher

It's a beautiful day
in the neighborhood...

— Mr. Rogers —

We had very limited access to substitute teachers at Berkshire Farm. The rural location and the reputation of our student clientele kept us at the bottom of the list of where substitutes were willing to work. To deal with the lack of substitutes, an absent teacher's classes were often covered by other Berkshire Farm teachers during their planning periods.

I substituted whenever I could. I was more than willing to cover a colleague's class. The pay was good and we struggled to manage at home as a single income family.

Subject final exams were given in the school auditorium. I was asked to fill in for Mr. Friedman's eighth grade science exam. Pete the Duty Officer was also assigned to the auditorium during exam week to assist with monitoring.

Friedman gave me his directions the day before. They were simple, "Most of the kids will finish early, but you have to keep them in the auditorium until the bell rings. Make sure they sign the declaration. And as you collect the exams, keep them in alphabetical order for me."

"I can handle that, Bob." I responded confidently. "Did the same thing for my English exam yesterday."

The next day, while Pete and I were walking to the auditorium, I informed him of Mr. Friedman's directions, "Sounds like Bob. By the book. We better not mess up. Why don't I make sure they sign the declaration and you put the exams in alphabetical order as they hand them to you. And make sure you sign the substitute log in the office to get your extra money."

The process of writing exams for students at The Farm was always a challenge because of the wide spectrum of reading levels within a class. A student could know the right answer but never comprehend the question. Each of the fill-in-the-blank questions on Bob Friedman's test were intentionally written in the simplest of sentences.

The teachers at Berkshire Farm framed their questions with the most elementary language. But even that consideration could sometimes confuse and generate the wrong answer.

Raoul from the Bronx was the last student to finish the exam. He raised his hand as instructed when his test was completed.

"Did you sign your declaration, Raoul?" asked Pete.

"Done. *I do so declare.* Just like Friedman taught us."

"Good. Now hand your exam to Mr. Weinlein."

Raoul lumbered up the aisle with his test. "Done, Mr. Weinlein. Finally done."

I glanced over Raoul's exam to make certain all parts were completed. I noticed one very strange response to question number seventeen:

Name a single celled organism ___________

I imagined Friedman toiling to compose that question in the simplest form. "Hold on a second, Raoul." I checked through some other test papers. The other students answered the question correctly: *amoeba*.

But not Raoul. His answer to question seventeen was beyond unusual.

I had to ask Raoul about his answer. "Did you look over your test carefully, Raoul? And answered all the questions just the way you wanted to? Like question seventeen, you want that to be your answer?"

"Like I said, Mr. Weinlein...I'm done."

"OK." I was perplexed. "Go back to your seat until the bell rings."

When the annoyingly loud Berkshire Farm bell rang, I held the auditorium door open as the students rushed out. Raoul was in no hurry. He moseyed on up to the exit door. I gestured to him with his exam paper. "Wait a minute, Raoul. I want to ask you something." I pointed again to his answer to question seventeen. "Are you sure you want to leave that for your answer?"

"Hell yeah, Mr. Weinlein. That's the deal."

"Really? Are you being a wise guy, Raoul? Why did you write '*Tino*' in your answer to *name a single celled organism?"*

"I wrote '*Tino*' because that's my answer." Raoul stared at me with big brown, inquisitive eyes, "What's the problem with that answer?"

"Because the correct answer is *amoeba*. Can you explain why '*Tino*' is your answer? No one else put that for their answer."

"Dig. I was thinking about that question real hard." Raoul looked down at question seventeen in the test booklet. "And then I decided...if my Momma got me one of those single celled things, that's what I'd name it...*Tino*."

CHAPTER TWENTY-NINE

Great American Folk Heroes

Rosa Parks showed us all that one little person can make a whole bunch of noise without as much as a whisper.

— Richard Pryor —

The academic departments at Berkshire Farm were blessed with an accommodating budget when ordering classroom materials. I was in the windowless bookroom with Jim, another English teacher. "The boys like these stories," he suggested handing me a paperback, *Great American Folk Tales.* "Mini biographies. High interest. Low reading level."

"Thanks. I'll give this a go," I flipped through the pages of the soft cover text.

"Just remember your class is fluid, Gregg. Changing all the time with the addition or departure of students. You will finally find yourself settled with a group of boys, and all of a sudden a new student is added or one leaves. And then it's a new ball game all over again. One student can change the whole dynamic of a classroom. So remember when choosing materials, shorter is always better than longer works of literature."

"Are you given advance notice when a student is added or removed from class?"

"You are. You are." Jim smiled mischievously. "Usually a knock on the door from the Duty Officer. You get a few seconds advance notice." He grinned sarcastically. "You think that'll be enough time for you?"

And so I began my career teaching eighth graders folk legends like John Henry, Paul Bunyan, and Davy Crockett. And Jim was right. The stories were perfect for my class.

For the unit assessment, my students had a choice whether to take a final test, write an essay about their favorite folk legend, or do a presentation on a legend not included in the text.

Willie-T raised his hand and asked, "Can I do my presentation on this Southern dude who ain't a folk legend but he gonna be. My pops says so. Can I do it 'bout him? I have his record. He be telling a story like nobody else. Even better than you, Mr. Wiiiiiiine - Liiiiiii-ine." There was a poetic rhythm to my student's elongated version of my name. "What'd you call the dudes telling the story, Teach?"

I provided my student with the literary term. "The narrator, Willie-T. Do you have the record here?"

"Yo. I got it here."

"At your cottage?"

"Yeah…and this dude *narrators* the stories so cool and he be so funny too. And the dude's a black man, Mr. Wiiiiine - Liiiiiine. And you know, my people is outnumbered in that legends book we reading. My pops gave me the record during my last home visit. He said it was my present for going away again." The class erupted in laughter.

"You can bring the record in and do your presentation tomorrow. But I still want you to write a short summary and hand that in on Monday. You can't just play a record for your grade. That wouldn't be fair to your classmates. You can write about why you think this person has the goods to become a legend."

There was excitement in Willie-T's voice as he spoke. "After class tomorrow we all gonna know 'bout the next great American folk legend. And you gonna be givin' me an A+, Mr. Wiiiine-Liiiine."

"We'll see. That will be determined by your presentation and your paper."

"You got it, Teach. Pops gonna be so proud when I tell him I got to use his record for my school project."

The next morning Willie-T sauntered into class carrying an LP titled, "Is It Something I Said?" I moved the metal audio cart to the front of the room.

"OK Willie-T, the stage is yours. I hope you have an introduction for us."

My student put the vinyl onto the record player and faced his fellow students. "This be Richard Pryor. He gonna be a future legend and he narrators the legend. See Mr. W? I used that word you taught us. This be the story about Mudbone."

"That's it for the introduction, Willie-T?"

"Not much else to tell, Mr. Wiiiiine-Liiiiiiine. The man speaks for himself. And he speaks for all of us. You gonna see."

Willie-T put the needle on the disc. The narrator began with a slow Southern drawl accented with imaginary chews on a wad of tobacco. *This is a story about...*"

I listened. I mean I lasted for only a few minutes. I rushed to lock my door. The class was melting down with raucous laughter.

I ran to the back of the classroom and closed the windows.

I ran to the media cart. I was crying with laughter. A silly image for a teacher. I pulled the needle off the record. I was in comic shock at the gut punching vulgarity. "What are you doing, Willie-T!? I can't have that playing in class. Jesus!" (Yes. I needed divine intervention.) "You'll get me fired! All I need is for Esther or Percy to walk in. I mean Mrs. Boughton or Mr. Martins. And I'll be fired. Gone." I took the vinyl off the player and handed it to Willie-T. "Don't bring this to school again. Take your record back to your cottage and keep it there."

"That's cold, Teach." He refused to take the disc from my hand. Willie-T was disappointed. "I ain't taking the record. You bring it home and play it. You listen to it and then tell me this dude ain't the funniest man on earth. He tells the truth about life. Tells you what life's 'bout. Says what's really going down. You gonna learn a lot 'bout life like you never know'd, Mr. Wiiiiine-Liiiiiiine"

Willie-T seemed sad. But he was serious about his request for me to listen to his record at home. I didn't argue with my student. Nor did I try to reason with him about my classroom response. I was genuinely shocked at the vulgar language I heard in just the first few minutes. But I didn't want to come across as a teacher who made judgements. I had enough of that dished out on me when I was a teenager.

I needed to reign in my class. The students were in hysterics despite the little they heard about Mudbone. But all I thought of was the principal or assistant principal walking into my classroom and hearing Willie-T's record.

I set the record on my dining room table when I got home and wondered if Willie-T was just being a wiseass in my class. Or was there something on the record that would make my student believe Richard Pryor should have a spot in American folklore?

After dinner I opened a can of beer and decided to give Willie-T's record a spin. I added an extension cord to my headphones and sat on a chair in the living room.

I laughed uncontrollably.

Constantly. My stomach hurt because I laughed so hard.

In tears, I listened to Richard Pryor unveil his tales of "...what life's 'bout." I knew of Bill Cosby. And I watched Redd Foxx on *Sanford and Son*. But I had never heard of Richard Pryor. And I never heard tales of such dysfunctions in life, economic imbalance, crazy relationships, social inequity, class disparity, and racism encased in such brilliant humor that the jokes enlightened as well as shocked.

Pryor's comedy was different, packed with brilliant unique sociological and insightful universal perspectives. His humor was insanely wild. His delivery and impersonations of characters were *over the top* and spot on. No race was exempt from his precise and insanely comic graphic depictions of people. His humor penetrated the soul and pierced the human psyche, allowing us to laugh at each other - *and especially at ourselves:*

"If they had like an Ethnic IQ test
You know the Chinese gonna win
Any mother-f..... eat with two sticks got to win"

For me, Richard Pryor created *one world* of massively imperfect human beings trying to carve out an existence despite their character flaws and society's injustices:

"I went to jail for income tax invasion
I didn't know a mother-f...... thing about no taxes
I told the judge, 'Your honor, I forgot.'
'You'll remember next year!' the judge told me.
You go down there looking for justice
That's what you find...
Just us."

Despite the off-the-wall insanity of Richard Pryor's humor, I suppose it was equally crazy that the comedian became a major influence in my life. I was a beginning "white folk" teacher in a predominantly minority school setting and Pryor had as much impact on my life as any singer I ever listened to, or any author I ever read.

Regardless of our own individual failures and the unfair life challenges thrown at us, and despite the one step forward but going nowhere existence so many of us live, and despite the absurdity of promises and dreams that never materialize, Richard Pryor taught me the power of laughter as a form of resilience. More than any musical hero, or any literary influence, Richard Pryor shaped my philosophy of life.

I listened to the whole album Willie-T assigned to me.

Willie-T…I owe you. And yes…you aced the project: A+…even before your essay summary.

A few years after my introduction to Richard Pryor, long after Willie-T was discharged from Berkshire Farm and never to be heard of again, I saw an ad in the *Arts & Leisure* section of the *NY Times:* ***Richard Pryor Live at Carnegie Hall.***

I purchased a ticket and took the Greyhound bus to NYC.

Over the years I have been to so many concerts and other forms of live entertainment: Dylan, Leonard Cohen, Springsteen, Bob Marley, and U2. And I attended readings by many poets and novelists, and I sat at numerous theatrical performances. In college I even took a trip to the Felt Forum in Madison Square Garden to attend a major literary event featuring the Russian poet, Yevgeny Yevtushenko. But no one was more memorable to me than seeing Richard Pryor in person at Carnegie Hall.

On show day I walked to my seat in the orchestra section and had this strange thought: could Willie-T be here with his father? He did live in Brooklyn.

"Excuse me," I said repeatedly maneuvering my way to my seat, "Excuse me, please." I was the only white person in the row of Richard Pryor fans.

Pryor was manic onstage and like no other performer I ever experienced. Our seats shook with the constant roar of laughter. Unlike his recordings, I witnessed his characters come to life in all their deranged beauty. Tears formed in my eyes. I had to catch my breath between outbursts of uncontrollable laughter. I shared my explosions of laughter with everyone else in the audience.

When Richard Pryor made an observation about the sold out audience that could have made me feel uncomfortable, I also erupted in laughter. I couldn't pause my laughter long enough to see if I felt uncomfortable. Richard Pryor prowled the massive stage. The manic comedian walked back to his microphone. He stared into the audience and observed, "Shortage of white people here."

My laughter could not be contained. A black woman sitting next to me nudged my arm and said, "That's you, Boy. And you's laughing."

And we kept laughing together for the entire show.

I often thought of writing to Richard Pryor. But he became a star and had his own TV show and appeared in several hit movies. I decided my letter would never reach him. I wanted to tell him how his humor stayed with me throughout my life. I wanted to tell him that I purchased all his records as soon as they were released. I wanted to tell him how he changed and shaped my perspective on life.

And I wanted to tell him how this young white teacher, living in the small town of Chatham, New York, was turned on to his brilliance by one of my eighth grade students who was sent to a delinquent school where I taught.

Even after Richard Pryor died, I thought of writing to his wife to let her know of the influence her husband had on my life. But I never did. And every time I think that I wish I had written, a sense of regret descends upon me.

The Carnegie Hall experience of being a minority sitting *alone* with a wildly raucous Richard Pryor audience will remain permanently engraved in my memory bank.

Leaving the theater still laughing with the others exiting onto 7th Avenue, I realized I was *never* really sitting *alone.* We all laughed together, imperfect human beings who recognized a fragment of ourselves in each of Richard Pryor's characters.

I walked over Forty-Second Street to the Port Authority bus terminal. At an all night market I picked up two sixteen ounce cans of beer for my three hour ride home.

On the bus I thought about the different races detailed and mimicked on the canvas of Richard Pryor's performance. So many people. So many sketches.

And I thought about my presence in the predominantly black audience.

And I realized for one brilliant evening at Carnegie Hall color was without color. Despite the *"shortage of white people."*

My most important teacher influence and life coach: Richard Pryor.

Thanks again Willie-T.

CHAPTER THIRTY

Visit From State Education Department

In the midst of movement and chaos
Keep stillness inside of you.

— Deepak Chopra —

Besides my initiation into the world of Richard Pryor, a visit from the NYS Department of Education also remains in my memory bank of Berkshire Farm. Funding for Berkshire Farm was mostly from both state and federal governments. Oversight for the school component was from the NYS Department of Education. Visits from that agency were infrequent but not unexpected. I remember vividly one visit to my classroom by a team of State Education bureaucrats.

I took pride in "the look" of my classroom for my students. Posters of literary giants like Nikki Giovanni, Judy Blume, and Toni Morrson were displayed on my walls. And on two large cork boards I pinned 8x10 black and white photos of writers, actors, sports heroes, singers, and musical groups.

At the time I was writing for a local arts paper and a sports weekly. Through my freelance assignments, I had contacts with public relations departments in the entertainment, sports, and book publishing industries. On occasion I would write to those contacts requesting publicity material to display in my classroom. Some of the photos and posters sent were enhanced by personalized autographs.

Whenever I picked up my mail in the main office and saw a package with a return address from Capitol Records, or the Buffalo Bills, or the Knicks, or the Yankees, I beamed with excitement knowing the contents would thrill my students. I always let my students open the large envelopes. One day a package arrived with a return address of Madison Square Garden. Inside was a personally autographed photo from a Knicks' superstar who was a favorite of my students, "To the Boys at Berkshire Farm - Walt 'Clyde' Frazier."

On my desk in a stand-up frame, I also placed a publicity photo of Joan Valentina. My students loved the background story of our friendship. Joan and I became close friends during our time together at the Spencertown Academy. She was an African-American actress and playwright from New York City who was part of an artist's residency in the quiet hillside town in Columbia County. And I taught a creative writing class for adults at the Academy.

I attended Joan's theatrical performances at Spencertown and she attended the readings by my students. In subsequent years I also went to her performances in the city. We remained long distance friends despite only seeing each other occasionally. One special memory of our friendship was a U2 concert at the Garden. We sat together in fantastic seats organized by friends in Ireland.

Some of my students were surprised by my close connection with Joan. Racial stereotypes prevailed on the city streets where my students grew up. Intrigued by our friendship, whenever I told my students I was going to NYC, the one question always asked was, "Are you going to see Joan?"

Needless to say, when the three bureaucrats from the Department of Education visited, I was certain they would be impressed by my decorated classroom and the connection made with my students.

At the end of the school day Peter the Duty Officer walked into my room, "Esther wants to see you now. She didn't say why but the women from State Ed are with her."

Esther's door was open but I still knocked, "Come in, Gregg." The agency representatives were in chairs circling the principal's desk. I was offered an open seat next to my principal. "Our guests from State Ed would like to talk to you about your classroom."

I'm sure I concocted a confident facial expression to ask *what's up?*

"Mr. Weinlein," the first bureaucrat stated, "to be perfectly blunt, we don't want our minority students aspiring to be only sports and music stars." I was taken off guard.

"Those are pipe dreams we shouldn't be promoting to our African-American students," added bureaucrat number two.

"We think you should remove the posters and photos," suggested the third member of the trinity of bureaucrats.

I sat aghast and in disbelief. I took a deep breath. "I'm sorry you have that perspective." My hands were on the side of the chair but I felt my fists clench. "My classroom walls *do not, and are not intended to,* suggest 'pipe dreams' to my students. There is a whole spectrum of life and careers displayed on my walls. And many are not professional athletes or musicians. There are authors, Nobel Prize winners, civil rights leaders, scientists, political leaders - a vast world I want my students to know exists and that they can be a part of. I made the effort to get those posters and photos, several which are personally autographed. And to my students, those pictures let them know they matter. I want them to know other adults, their heroes, will still connect and take the time to let the Berkshire Farm boys know they're not forgotten. Did you talk with any of my students about what they thought or felt about them?"

Bureaucrat number one seemed flustered by my response and my attitude. But I wasn't caving. Picking up her large leather bag off the office floor, she reiterated, "Our recommendation is they come off your wall."

But I still wanted to take my shots. I never had respect for bureaucrats who dictate from a distance to the actual work environment.

"And should I take down the poster of Nikki Giovanni because I wouldn't want any of the boys aspiring to be a poet? And what about the poster of Doctor King? And the movie poster of Sidney Poitier? God help us if the boys ever desired an acting career."

Like sheep, the other two bureaucrats picked up their oversized bags and walked towards the door. The most obnoxious of the group turned and said, "Redo your walls. Classrooms should be about education."

As they walked out I said sarcastically, "And I bet you don't believe education is enhanced in a classroom where students want to be? Have a wonderful day." I turned back in my chair and looked at my principal. "So much for academic freedom. Those people didn't even speak to my students. They know nothing about the boys and still they spit out a demand that is only going to tick off a group of teenage boys. Useless petty bureaucrats."

Esther finally spoke, "Gregg, no one here questions your dedication to your students. You are always there for the boys. Your students know that and respect you for that."

"I don't care about that now, Esther. I mean I appreciate the comment and I apologize for my anger and attitude. But that meeting was sick. I never expected that. What's next?"

Esther didn't answer me. She looked at me with a sad but authoritative calmness in her eyes. She didn't respond verbally. I knew her response by reading her face: *my hands are tied.*

Before my students entered the classroom the next morning, the decorations were off the wall. I didn't tell my students why everything was taken down but campus gossip got the word out. Students appeared at my doorway. Many were not even my students but they still participated in an avalanche of angry responses:

"That's bullshit, Mr. Weinlein," Marcus said. "Nasty bitches. You see the way they look down at us when they here."

"Fuck'em," said an older student slapping the wall. "Who were they? They ain't got no right to tell you what to do. It ain't their classroom."

"Yeah. It's our classroom too, Mr. Weinlein," noted Big George. "Don't listen to them."

"I saw them waddle into school. Old white bitches," Jerome added. "What they even know about us?"

On Friday I was asked again to stop by the main office after school. Brian the supervisor of cottage coordinators was there along with assistant principal Percy Martins. Also present was Lorraine, the teacher union president and the English Department chairperson, Marion.

Esther spoke first. "I do not think anyone anticipated the uproar your classroom issue would cause. The students are still very upset."

Brian added, "I've never witnessed the boys so united in their anger like they have been this past week. I told Esther this morning their anger is not only while in school, but also spilling out throughout the campus. They see this as *the system dictating* again against them."

Lorraine spoke, "We think you should put everything back up on your walls. The State Ed directive was without educational purpose. I know you are still angry, Gregg, but State Ed only visits once or twice a year. Some years they don't even visit. And you know that I'm not a fan of State Ed. I think they come out here to justify their jobs."

"Gregg, it is not only you and your students who are upset," Esther acknowledged. "And you're right Lorraine, it is a rare occasion that the state visits. And they always give us notice when they are coming."

"So?" I asked with my head down talking to the floor.

"Well...if you are willing," Lorraine continued sarcastically, "when Paul Revere informs us they're coming, you take everything down again and then put everything back up when they leave. And we'll all help. We know your students want everything back on the walls."

"And it is also a valuable lesson for the boys," Percy Martins added. "The anger will subside and they will see that an alternative solution was worked out without being destructive. A little game playing maybe...but we're all here for our students. And the boys will respect that."

I smiled in agreement and appreciation. "I guess I have my weekend plans. I'll put everything back up by Monday morning. Thank you."

I drove back out to The Farm on Saturday and Sunday.

When my students arrived Monday morning, their classroom had been redecorated.

To this day I only have to flashback to this incident early in my career to understand why I distrust and dislike large bureaucracies.

CHAPTER THIRTY-ONE

Ricky's Home Leave

No one knows what it's like...
to be the sad man
behind blue eyes

— Peter Townsend —

Little Ricky remains my saddest memory of my seven years at Berkshire Farm. He was the smallest, shyest, most polite, most respectful, and most appreciative student in any of my classes. All the street smart, badass attitudes projected by most of the other boys were missing from him.

At home Little Ricky was frequently truant and a chronic shoplifter. Despite several PINS appearances in family court, and years on juvenile probation, his attendance at school never improved nor was he able to rid himself of his "sticky fingers." But he was a good student at Berkshire Farm. Focused in class. Always did his homework. Even studied.

Near the classroom flag in the front of the room were two large bulletin boards where I posted homework due dates, quiz dates, life skills quotes, articles, and student recognition certificates.

Ricky was always the first to finish assignments and tests. One day when I was updating the bulletin board in my room he asked, "Mr. Weinlein? I can help you with the board after school."

"Thanks, Ricky. But you have your activity at the cottage after school."

"I know...but if you stay after school with a teacher they don't care if you don't go back to the cottage. You just have to give me a permission slip."

"I appreciate the offer, Ricky." I took down a Nikki Giovanni poem and replaced it with Maya Angelou's poem, *Still Rise.* "But I think I would feel guilty if you missed your activities to help me."

Ricky wore large wire rim glasses with thick frames. "I'd rather stay here and help you than be at the cottage. Mrs. Smith lets me stay after for Math help but she's absent today. I'd do a good job, Mr. Weinlein."

Such an emotionally downcast fourteen year old. I thought to myself that Ricky was likely an easy target to be bullied by the bigger students. "Sure, Ricky. I could use the help. Let me sign a note for you."

Throughout the year the boys could earn a "home leave" which were extended weekends scheduled once a month for students to visit their families. Boys who did not accumulate a certain number of negative "conduct points" were granted the privilege of going home from Thursday through Sunday. A home leave was the most sought after incentive for the boys, making the conduct report system an effective deterrent to limit misbehavior.

Little Ricky didn't get conduct reports. Instead he got recognition certificates. In April, Ricky was on the list of boys who earned a home leave. No one was surprised. But the day before his bus was to leave Berkshire Farm, an incident occurred in my classroom that left both staff and students in shock.

Little Ricky always sat in the front row. Not just in my class, but in all his classes. Seconds before the bell rang to end class, he stood from his seat and walked to the back of the room. He stood over Leon's desk. Leon was a sixteen year old eighth grader. A manchild.

One of the biggest and toughest boys at The Farm. Without hesitation, Little Ricky cold cocked Leon with a sucker punch and knocked his classmate out of his seat onto the floor.

I was in disbelief. The class was stunned. I followed classroom protocols and called the office for immediate assistance. The Duty Officer and other staff members arrived quickly. As they rushed into my room, I was struggling to restrain Leon who had gotten himself off the floor and wanted to get Ricky.

The adult response to major incidents at The Farm was always swift and impressive. Leon was pinned against the brick classroom wall by the Duty Officer and two staff members. Ricky was dragged out of my room by a cottage social worker who was at the school, "Good job, Ricky. Now you lost your home visit."

Leon was ballistic. Screaming obscenities laced with threats of what he was going to do to Ricky. Finally the staff members managed to escort Leon from my classroom.

I retreated to my desk and crumbled into my chair in confused silence. Bewildered and feeling inept, I was speechless. There was never a fight in my classroom. But today there was an unexpected assault.

Throughout the day, Percy Martins went to each classroom and informed the teachers of an emergency staff meeting after school. No one was surprised. News of Ricky's attack became the buzz of the school.

At the meeting, Esther introduced Doctor Bell and said our school psychiatrist would provide an update including information about Ricky that sparked his violent action.

This faculty meeting had an air of attentiveness that was usually lacking in our monthly meetings with Doctor Bell. We were aware of the Doctor's impressive credentials and his psychological insights were to be admired. But when he spoke there was always a snicker or a whispered mimicking of his mumbled, heavily accented evaluations.

And you thought all teachers were professional and respectful? Wrong!

Today we all listened carefully and with interest and concern.

Doctor Bell informed us, "We will revisit the milieu of treatment and intervention for Ricky Wilson. He won't be going home. He will remain in his cottage for the next week supervised throughout the day and evening. He will not be in school for a week. Ricky will have formal meetings with his social worker twice a day. Every day he will meet with our medical team. I already met with Ricky for over an hour. We will continue to meet every day during his restrictions."

"And what's the deal with Leon?" asked Bill, one of our gym teachers. "He's gonna wanna beat the crap out of Ricky." (I don't know if it is a gym teacher syndrome but Bill always spoke without a sense of professionalism.) "Leon will make mincemeat out of Ricky."

Principal Esther responded, "We spoke with Leon's probation officer. She thinks it would be best if we let Leon keep his home leave since he was the victim. Ricky and Leon won't be on campus together for the long weekend. His PO will monitor Leon and arrange for him to be counseled while home."

I raised my hand. I seldom spoke at faculty meetings. "Doctor Bell - you said you met with Ricky this afternoon?"

"Yes. A long discussion. Ricky is sorry for what he did. He wants me to apologize to you for his actions. He accepts his punishments."

"I'm glad for all that, Doctor. But *why*? He just got out of his seat and decked Leon. Did he give you a reason? Because we are all shocked that he did that to Leon."

"Yes," the psychiatrist answered. "I was able to derive his motivation. Ricky felt cornered. The boy saw no other action to bail himself out." There was a pause in the Doctor's response.

"Can you share with us why?" I wanted more information.

"Confidentiality is an issue but I can tell you what can be derived from school placement reports, court reports, and assessments from the Department of Probation and Social Services."

"I think we would all be grateful if you shared your insights, Doctor Bell." I was anxious to learn about my student.

"Some things Ricky shared with me I am bound by confidentiality. But I will connect the dots for you based on what I can share. Ricky grew up in an abusive home - even when he was living with relatives. He trusted no one. He was always fearful which limited his social growth and contributed to his truancy issues. His shoplifting gave him an unhealthy sense of control and escape. And some of those shoplifting crimes were the result of orders to steal from adults he was living with at the time."

"But Doctor," noted Emma, a Science teacher, "all of our students have seriously dysfunctional home lives and they don't go around attacking other students in the classroom for no reason."

"In Ricky's mind he had a justifiable reason," Dr. Bell continued. "He was anxious and extremely nervous about his home leave tomorrow. Unlike the other boys who are excited to go home. Ricky was afraid. He wanted a way out without admitting he didn't want to be home. He wasn't going to say, 'I don't want to take my home leave because my family has screwed me over.' He was looking for a way out that would *save face* on campus. So he attacked Leon and had his home leave revoked. Ricky was going to do whatever it took to *not go home*."

We left the faculty meeting touched by the motivation behind Ricky's uncharacteristic action. My teacher's motto to my friends has always been *I have a life at school, and I have a life outside of school.* And now I realized so do all my students. But sometimes that life outside of school for my students at The Farm was complicated and fractured by abuse.

I realized after that meeting, if I was going to be the teacher I wanted to be, I had *to know* the life of my students outside of school.

CHAPTER THIRTY-TWO

AWOLs

I work all day
I work all night
To pay the bills
I have to pay

— ABBA —

I packed my gym bag filled with papers and quizzes to grade during the evening. Pete stopped me in the main lobby and asked, "Any plans for tonight?"

"Just grading all these," I answered, lifting my gym bag to show him the folders.

"Hey, If you can grade them riding shotgun, you can add five hours on the clock and earn some extra money." Pete sat casually on top of the duty officer desk counting the cigarettes in his box of Marlboro.

"How's that?" I politely asked, knowing I wasn't interested in giving up my evening at home.

"The cops picked up Tony Jones this morning. He went AWOL last night. Guess his freedom didn't last long, right?" He closed his smokes and put the pack in his shirt pocket. "But he did get further than most of our other AWOLs. A good distance. He's sitting at the police station in Utica."

I didn't know Tony well. He was older than my students. "So what's the extra cash? What's involved?"

"A road trip out to Utica. We put Tony in the back seat. Lock the doors. And drive him back to The Farm. Easy money. We bring Tony back, complete a voucher, and you get five hours of extra pay in your next check. No expenses for us. We even get money for food on the way out."

I thought for a moment. The proposition did sound like easy money that I shouldn't be turning down. "And I can grade these in the car?" Pete nodded. "What time do you leave?"

"If you're game, we can leave now. Easy money, Gregg. The job is a piece of cake: you grade your tests and I listen to my eight tracks. My usual shotgun partners are going to the hoop game tonight against Pittsfield. So I'm scraping the bottom of the barrel asking you."

"Thanks for the confidence in me." I responded smiling. "Let me call home. If everything is okay there, then I'm good to go."

We always had a few AWOLs from Berkshire Farm. But not as many as you would think for an unlocked and unguarded facility. The lack of success was the result of constant messaging about our extraordinarily high rate of AWOL returns, along with the reality that the next home leave privilege would immediately be revoked. The message was consistent, *it's not worth taking a chance.*

The boys who did go AWOL simply bolted off campus to the two main highways outside Berkshire Farm - Route 22 or Route 295. Their escape was generally short-lived. State or local police would usually pick up the boys in less than an hour. But Tony, making his way to Utica, that was a big deal.

The staff also created AWOL tall-tales to deter the boys from running away: the terrors of The Berkshire Mountains. Although going over the mountains was the more logical escape route, the staff spun frightening stories that made the boys so fearful of the mountain journey, they opted to run out to the main highways.

How the Berkshire Mountains prevented AWOLs remains a humorous memory. Our boys were "*bad*" kids. I mean *real bad.* Tough as hell. Juvenile delinquents from the violent streets of New York's largest cities. A few of our teenagers had a history of gang assaults. Some had weapons charges over them. Many had substance abuse problems and others worked as "mules" delivering drugs. At a young age they had been indoctrinated into the criminal world. They were street-smart and wore a mask of fearlessness.

Except when it came to the Berkshire Mountains. The tall-tales authored by the staff included stories of bears and foxes roaming throughout the mountains behind the school. We embellished the tales with vivid descriptions of poisonous snakes and insects. And we graphically detailed how these desperate creatures were always looking for new prey - especially teenage boys.

Sure violence was prevalent in the lives of our boys. But not like the violence of young males being viciously attacked by predators in the mountains. So instead of escaping into Massachusetts by hiking over the Berkshires, the boys were picked up by the police on a highway just outside The Farm.

In my memory bank I created a humorous scenario of two boys in their cottage contemplating their AWOL from The Farm:

AWOL Boy #1: "We'll sneak out after the last bed check."

AWOL Boy #2: "Which way we going?"

AWOL Boy #1: "Out to the highway and hitch a ride."

AWOL Boy #2: "Why not split over the mountain? We'd be in Massachusetts."

AWOL Boy #1: "Yo...you fuckin' crazy? I ain't gonna get ate up by no bear!"

CHAPTER THIRTY-THREE

The Queechy Queen Lunch Time Cruise

The sun is shining
and the weather is sweet

— Bob Marley —

"Where the hell is Tom?" Eddie yelled to us as we high stepped through the cold waters of Queechy Lake to board his boat. We ran past Emily and Lynn, two other teachers having their lunch at a picnic table. Our pant legs were rolled up to our knees. We carried chips, sandwiches, and Wickzy had boxes of Friehofers chocolate chip cookies and glazed donuts for dessert. "We can't wait forever for Tommy."

"He went to get his cooler." I answered climbing onto the Queechy Queen.

"We gotta get moving." Eddie noted. "We don't get the whole afternoon for lunch."

"Here I come!" Tommy called splashing through the waters. "I'm coming. I got the beer." He held up a plastic cooler for evidence and reached out his other hand for help getting onto the boat.

"Jesus...Tommy! Your pants are drenched." Roger noted. "They'll still be wet when you get back to class."

Tommy dropped himself into a cushioned seat. The boat shook, adjusting to the weight of his stocky body. He looked up to the heavens brushing the water off his cuffed chinos, "Shit - with this sunshine they'll dry out in no time."

On the last Friday in June we skipped our basketball game to celebrate surviving another school year. Eddie's family owned a lake house and a boat which he commandeered for our special event.

"You got your tapes, Gregg? I got the boombox." Roger pulled a large eight track player out of his bag.

Eddie shut down the engine and we drifted out from the shoreline. We rocked gently in the middle of Queechy Lake. The reggae backbeats of the Wailers grooved from the speakers as Bob Marley sang, "*There's a natural mystic blowing through the air.*"

On this warm afternoon with brilliant sunshine, Eddie's boat danced to the hypnotic rhythms. Tommy handed a can of Schaefer beer to each of the teachers. (I know - how dare teachers drink a beer during their lunch hour! I'm sure teachers don't imbibe today.)

We ate our sandwiches and polished off the cookies. Conversation was at a minimum. After finishing our beers we put the empties back into Tommy's cooler, closed our eyes, and listened to Marley's *Exodus* album.

I remember hearing, "Waiting in Vain." But I didn't hear the whole song. I fell asleep.

Our peaceful lunch was shattered by frantic screams from the shoreline.

Emily and Lynn waved their arms in wildly animated gestures and yelled out our names at the top of their voices.

Roger heard them first, "What the hell is wrong with them? Jesus! Like two crazy banshees. Look at them, Eddie." Roger was shaking Eddie's shoulder to wake him up.

"Jesus Christ!" Tommy exclaimed without praying. He jumped up from his seat pointing to his watch. "It's 12:50! We got ten minutes to class."

Eddie moved quickly to start the engine. "For Christ's sake." All of a sudden five teachers became very religious. "Jesus" was the dominant declaration in our heavenly petition. Eddie gunned the boat towards the shore.

Emily and Lynn continued to call out, "Hurry. You're going to be late for class." And then they turned and ran towards the school.

We stood on the Queechy Queen leaning forward as if we could make the boat move faster. We adjusted our school attire, tucked in our shirts, and rolled our pants up again. Jumping into the shallow waters, we galloped back to school.

"This is going to be a fast break like we never ran in hoop," I said, leading the dash up the dirt road.

"Yeah," Roger added, "we'll run our asses off and we'll still be screwed for being late."

The bell rang as we passed the farmland and entered the faculty parking area. I could only imagine what we looked like panting and stumbling, rushing back to our classrooms. But we were on a mission. Dedicated teachers. We had to get back to educating our students.

We were laughing and panting as we hit the final lap.

Tommy put our run into perspective, "Fuck it! We're three minutes late or ten minutes late…we're fucked either way."

Mark, a cottage supervisor, was there to greet us as we neared the entrance to the school. He laughed at his fellow Berkshire Farm professionals. "Slow down. Slow down. Tommy looks like he's gonna have a heart attack. Take it easy." We stopped running to catch our breath.

"The bell rang, didn't it?" I panicked, reaching out my arm to lean on Mark.

"Yeah. No problem," assured Mark in his soothing nonchalant counseling voice. "Percy and Ester are over at the Administration Building."

Tommy struggled to put his tie on. "Aren't the boys already in their classes?"

"Got it covered," Mark answered, still laughing at us. "Emily and Lynn told me the ETA for the Queechy Queen was late. I got you covered. I divided up the cottage staff bringing the kids back from lunch and assigned them to stay in your classes. And don't worry... when you get to your classroom you'll think you're walking into church. I told the staff to tell the boys if there is any noise, any problems, they lose their after school privileges for a week. You'll have a classroom of angels when you walk in."

CHAPTER THIRTY-FOUR

My Departure From Berkshire Farm

Can I sail through the changin' ocean tides?
Can I handle the seasons of my life?

— Stevie Nicks —

A few years after receiving my Berkshire Farm certificate and my award pin for five years of service, I felt myself conflicted by a desire to teach elsewhere at a secondary level in a non-residential public school.

I was never dissatisfied with my position at The Farm. I enjoyed my classes and my students. Each school day was an unpredictable adventure. And I appreciated the supportive environment with the staff and administration. We were a team working together to improve the quality of life for our troubled teens. And I loved our lunch time basketball games and the Queechy Queen cruises.

My teaching career began at The Farm right after graduating from the university. I had grown as a teacher. And as a person. I credit my growth to my years at Berkshire Farm. But now I was seeking a different educational experience.

There was no incident that motivated me to look for another position. Not the State Education visit. And not even the sad learning experience with Ricky. Those incidents did shape my teacher's philosophy. I realized I wanted my students to learn to take control over the many challenging aspects of their life. I wanted them to be resilient and to know they owned their future.

I wanted to teach my students to believe in themselves and to transcend the roadblocks that surfaced in their lives. I felt a connection between their teen years and my own. Afterall, I had *Been there / Taught that.*

I knew I wanted to continue working with at-risk adolescents. But after seven years at Berkshire Farm, I felt a desire to move on and explore new educational challenges for myself. Besides, I believed at-risk students were in every high school.

My writing and the creative writing classes I taught in Spencertown and Albany cleared my vision to understand my desire for another teaching position. Several short stories and poems of mine were published in literary magazines throughout the country. But the sense of achievement I felt from being published was shared only by Marion and Jim, two other English teachers at The Farm, and Roger the art teacher.

Not that I was looking for a "*congrats*" pat on the back, but my creative writing was a significant part of my existence. I felt that aspect of my life was closeted while working at The Farm.

I also ventured into playwriting during my third year at Berkshire Farm. I was reading extensively about recruiting scandals in college sports, especially an investigative report in the Washington Post. I also read the book, *Athletes For Sale.* I was inspired to write a script about the scandals. Each day after school, I went to the Chatham Bakery, consumed too much coffee, and wrote my play in a composition notebook. Six months later I finished writing, *Booker.*

The play revolved around a highly recruited high school basketball star and his proud family. All the characters in the play were African-American except for the criminal recruiters. My years working at The Farm helped me create authentic dialogue while incorporating a relevant dose of current slang.

Playwriting was a new genre for me. What does a playwright do once the script is written? Do you try to get the play staged? Are plays published? The process seemed overwhelmingly time consuming. And I feared being mired in creative quicksand if I devoted all my writing time to bringing my play to the next level. I had other writing projects spinning around in my head.

Besides, would a play about a black family written by a young white school teacher in his early twenties with the name "Weinlein," even be considered an appropriate literary effort? I didn't know. But I was certain I did not want to invest the time to learn about stage production or play publication.

Still, I did write a play. And I felt a sense of literary achievement with what I had written.

A writer's magazine listed a playwriting contest at a college in New Orleans. I knew I didn't want to undertake the time commitment to "shop" a play around for possible production, but a playwriting contest seemed to require less effort. Why not? A one shot deal. Package the manuscript and send off the submission.

Several months passed when I received a letter from the theater department. *Booker* was selected as a finalist for another round of readings.

Another month passed, and another formal letter. *Booker* was awarded third place. No staging of my basketball play. But for my literary soul and inspiration, *Booker* was a slam dunk.

There was no disappointment. I was informed nearly a hundred plays were submitted. Not bad, I told myself. Besides, I had already moved on from my playwriting venture. I was nearing completion of a manuscript for my first collection of poetry.

Playwriting ended for me with *Booker*. I never wrote another play. I loved creating dialogue and the thought of a literary genre dominated by characters speaking intrigued me. I concluded my playwriting venture was an effort to prove something to myself. Third place was enough.

To this day, *Booker* has occupied a spot in a very old metal filing cabinet in the garage.

My creative spirit existed off campus during my tenure at The Farm, especially my writer's workshop at the Spencertown Academy where I met Joan. What I found most inspirational at the Academy were the friendships with other artists at the retreat. Not just writers, but also actors and actresses. Some performers were from area community theaters and others, like Joan, were from as far away as New York City.

There was no literary camaraderie present at Berkshire Farm. Teaching was focused on remediation. The texts we utilized were mostly abridged editions of literature rewritten as low-level reading materials. I was teaching eighth and ninth grade and only a few of my students were reading at grade level. And many were reading at the third or fourth grade level.

I wondered what teaching would be like in a non-residential public school. I thought of how different my classes would be if my students were high school juniors or seniors, and not exclusively boys.

I also thought of how much I would enjoy teaching Hemingway, Faulkner, August Wilson, and poets like Dylan Thomas and Langston Hughes. I could also introduce my students to writers who were personal favorites of mine like C.P. Cavafy, H.D., and Harry Crews. Writers who were not included in typical literature textbooks. And of course I thought of the joy I would feel bringing my own published writings into my classroom. A sense of educational excitement flushed through me whenever I thought of teaching elsewhere.

I knew I would begin a new position with the realization that socially disadvantaged students were not exclusive to Berkshire Farm. I only needed to recall my days as a self destructive, dangerously at-risk teenager. I knew there were students with challenges like mine, and like those of the boys at Berkshire Farm, in every public school. And it was that sensitivity, insight, and understanding that carried me through for my entire teaching career.

I was also certain, having survived my teen years, and with all that I learned while at Berkshire Farm, I could guarantee my future students that their at-risk issues would never go unnoticed.

As these thoughts became more frequent, they soon transformed into dreams and a goal for myself.

I started to apply for other teaching positions.

CHAPTER THIRTY-FIVE

Columbia High School Job Interview

It's time to move on, time to get going,
What lies ahead, I have no way of knowing

— Tom Petty —

During the spring and summer of 1983, I began my search for a public school teaching position. I looked at postings in newspapers, networked with other educators, and spent hours after a graduate class at the University Placement Office.

I didn't find a position I was interested in during my searches at the university but I did publish a poem in The English Journal about that experience.

At The University Placement Office

A wooden box
on a metal table
captures carelessly
tossed papers

VACANCY NOTICE

A man, and a young woman
both quite young
read each paper
with eyes so tired
and so intense

They exchange one
for another
as if sharing the
possibility of some
dream to come true

In this room
two employees in cushioned
chairs casually watch a
soap opera on TV

So thin
yet so wide
is the distance between
wanting
and
having

For months I shot blanks looking for a public school position. And then, by mere coincidence, I saw an opening advertised in a small community newspaper. Columbia High School in East Greenbush was seeking a teacher to work with challenging students who were frequent discipline problems.

Did I think the position was right *up* my proverbial alley? I did. I was intrigued. I called the district administration center for more information. From my conversation with the administrative assistant in the Superintendent's Office, I sensed she thought my candidacy was noteworthy. Making the position even more appealing, I was now living in the East Greenbush Central School District.

I applied for the job. A few days later I received a call from Columbia High School to schedule an interview with the principal.

Charlie Patricia was recognized as a "country club" principal. His leadership style was down to earth, friendly, casual, and trusting of his staff to do their job. His hands off approach to school management was based on mutual respect and his belief, *we are all in this boat together.* And yet he was frantically explosive at any sign of professional incompetence or student misbehavior. He was known throughout the educational community for his helter-skelter authoritative outbursts over the PA.

I witnessed the frenzied characteristics of Charlie Patricia's principalship during my subsequent years at the school. But nowhere was his fiery unhinged personality apparent in my interview.

"So...SUNY/Albany to Berkshire Farm and now looking to be at Columbia High School." He held my application and resume in his hand. "Tell me about your work at Berkshire Farm."

"Sure. I finished my seventh year there in June. The students reside there. All boys. Teenagers who were sent there through the juvenile court system. I taught English. The different grade levels are on my application. The students were socially disadvantaged, or called at-risk, and in need of academic remediation, counseling, and support. They were from the larger cities in New York."

"We are hoping for someone with that background." The principal continued in a conversational manner sipping from his NY Giants coffee mug. "Do you know much about Columbia?" He didn't wait for my answer. "We're a suburban school, middle class families, but we have our own screw ups here. So your teaching experience made your resume stand out. The students you would be working with are predominantly discipline problems. Consistently in violation of our code of conduct. Some of our teachers refer to them as *frequent fliers*."

Our conversation lasted about twenty minutes. Mr. Patricia asked me if I'd be interested in coaching and told me there was a JV football position open. "If I am hired, Mr. Patricia, I really want to focus on my classroom responsibilities - especially for my first year. But if you don't get anyone else I can take on that position too." He seemed surprised that I didn't jump at the offer to coach.

Once the teaching aspect of my interview ended, the principal kept talking to me about football. And I learned why he was surprised at my lack of interest in coaching. He was a huge fan of the sport and I was about to find out *my* true identity was lost.

During the interview he called me by my brother's name.

"What we are trying to do here, Gary, is help the students who violate our code of conduct. And then they get suspended, which further impedes their education. The cycle goes on and on."

Another question went like this, "Some of these kids are a real pain in the ass, Gary. Do you see that being a problem if they are in your classroom?"

"I'm very familiar with that type of student. No problem on this end."

Charlie stood and shook my hand concluding the interview. "The next step will be a call from the Superintendent's office for their interview. Round two, Gary. But I'm an upfront guy and I am going to tell you right now that I will be recommending you for the position.

I hope you remain interested in the job because I think you will be a good fit here at Columbia High School."

"Thank you, Mr. Patricia. *I am definitely* interested and I would really like to be part of your school."

"Well...just get through the interview at the district office. The Superintendent has already commented on your background. And when you get the good news, because I'm confident you will, we have some more paperwork for you to complete at the high school. And that's when you stop with the, 'Mr. Patricia'. Just call me, Charlie. Got that, Gary?"

And that was my job seeking dilemma. And I had no knowledge on how to handle the situation. Do I correct and maybe embarrass the principal by telling him he keeps calling me "Gary" instead of my name? Do I just tell him "Gary" is my brother's name? I mean "Gregg" was in my cover letter. "Gregg" was typed on my resume. And I saw that he wrote *"Gregg - 9:30"* on his large desk calendar.

So why was Charlie Patricia calling me "Gary" instead of "Gregg"?

I was certain I knew the reason. My younger brother, Gary, was an acclaimed local football player at the time. Throughout the summer, he appeared on the sports pages of the local newspapers and was a frequent topic of talk radio sports shows. He also appeared on local television stations. At the time of my interview, soon after a stint with the Toronto Argonauts in the Canadian Football League, Gary was in California trying out for the San Francisco 49s.

Back to my dilemma. Do I correct the person who may be my future boss? Do I tell Charlie Patricia he has been calling me by my brother's name?

I copped out. I wanted the job so I decided if Charlie thinks he is hiring my brother to teach at Columbia High School then let him think he is hiring Gary. That's fine with me. I just wanted the job.

At the Superintendent's office many of the questions were similar to the ones asked by Charlie. In an effort to ascertain my ability to cope with what was perceived as a challenging discipline situation I was asked, "Gregg, suppose you walked into the boys' room and saw a student smoking...is that a scenario you would be comfortable handling?"

A big smile restrained itself from appearing on my face as I thought of the school discipline and legal problems with the boys at Berkshire Farm. Confidently, I answered, "I am certain that scene would not be a problem for me."

CHAPTER THIRTY-SIX

To Educate or Not to Educate: That Is the Question

All and all you're just another brick in the wall

In the late eighties and early nineties, school discipline was a frequent agenda item at faculty assemblies, board of education meetings, and even with the PTO. Suspension rates were closely monitored by the State Education Department, and school administrators were desperate to reduce discipline referrals that found habitual violators of the code of conduct being suspended.

The Assistant Superintendent invited me on a field trip to Greene County to visit a school district's alternative program. "We'll make this a quick tour," he said driving his silver Lexus LS south on the New York State Thruway. "Our goal is to get a read on if their alternative program helps the district by removing the students who are always in trouble at school."

I thought about his comment the entire ride: *"...helps the district"*. I wondered if there was any intention to help the student. The Director of School Business rode in the front seat. I sat in the back with the new high school principal who arrived after Charlie Patricia retired. From their conversation, I felt the program we were visiting sounded like the school at Berkshire Farm. Not residential, but isolated away from their home school.

The Greene County alternative program operated in a trailer converted into a classroom with two teachers and nine students. There wasn't much to observe. The East Greenbush administrators conversed with the teachers while I tried to engage with the students. Most students were put off by our visit as if *their turf* was being compromised, except for Donny who wore a Ramones shirt. He told me his name after I introduced myself and asked him about the punk rock band.

"I like your shirt. What's your favorite Ramones song?"

Donny smiled. "That's easy. When you gotta sit here all day and do nothing I like to sing to myself, *'I wanna be sedated.'* You know the Ramones?"

"I may be a teacher but I'm not that old yet," I answered smiling while I pulled up a card table chair next to Donny's desk. "Do you know the song, Pet Sematary?" Donny nodded without much enthusiasm. "I'm partial to that song. I'm an English teacher so I like the song's connection to Stephen King. Do you know the author, Stephen King?"

"Naaah. I don't read much. I'd rather play my guitar. Haven't read a school book since grade school. But I still made it to high school."

After only a few years at Columbia I was surprised to learn that many students, not just alternative education students, get through high school doing very little reading. Donny told me he doesn't like "what they tell me I gotta read in school to read." He lifted up his desk top and pulled out a stack of music magazines along with a copy of, *"No One Here Gets Out Alive."*

"Ok, Donny," I responded, pointing to the biography of Jim Morrison and the Doors. I guess you do read."

I thought of the milieu created at Berkshire Farm. A large gym with a large pool. Hoop courts at the cottages. And soundproof music rooms for the students to jam in Wickzy's classes. As those images flashed before me, and having spoken with Donny, I reminded myself of the huge gap in equity at public education and priorities in school budgeting. And I thought of all the monies budgeted for sports programs and the little that is even considered for students at-risk who tend not to be interested in sports.

"Do you mind if I ask you why you are here in the alternative school? We are starting a program where I teach and we are looking for information."

"Mostly just didn't go to school. I was on PINS and my probation officer was on my back all the time," Donny answered sincerely. "And I kept getting suspended. Then I got violated by my PO and the judge told me to attend the alternative school or I get sent away."

"Any particular reason you didn't go to school?"

"Didn't fit in. Not with the students. And not with the teachers there. And my grades sucked. And then I got behind even more every time I got suspended. And I kept getting suspended. I just gave up. And then I started smoking pot regularly. Like what else you gonna do if you're just hanging out."

I was surprised at Donny's willingness to share his story. "Do you live at home, Donny?"

"Yeah. With my mother and father."

"How are they doing with everything going on in your life?"

Donny smirked. "Doesn't matter. My mom travels for work and she ain't never around. And my Dad's drunk all the time. He doesn't have a clue if I'm supposed to be at school." Donny began to organize his reading materials.

"Will you be able to graduate from high school in this program?"

"Not sure. I don't do much school work here. But I got passing grades."

"What about your school counselor? Do you see the counselor in the alternative program?"

"Hell no. Even at the high school the only time I saw my counselor was to get my schedule. Or if there was a big meeting to get back into school after I got suspended. There ain't no counselors coming down to the trailer. *Outta sight outta mind.* But Brian and Ed are cool. Our teachers. We can talk with them if we need to."

On the way back to East Greenbush our discussion about the program was noteworthy. Differences in philosophies on school discipline became obvious, as was the concept and purpose for an alternative program at Columbia. Would the purpose of the alternative program be to help the at-risk students in our school? Or would the purpose be to isolate the discipline problems from the mainstream population?

Administrator One: "I guess a trailer program is one way to get the bad kids away from the students who come to school to learn."

Administrator Two: "I would be reluctant to add that expense to the school budget; the cost to buy and refurbish a trailer and to hire two teachers for only a dozen students. I don't think that would be an easy *sell* with the school board and the taxpayers."

Administrator Three: "We would have to promote the positive impact an alternative program would have at the high school. We could get our most disruptive students out of the mainstream and emphasize how that would improve the classroom atmosphere and benefit our other students."

All three administrators nodded in agreement. I sat quietly staring at the barbed wire fence as we passed the Coxsackie Prison visible from the New York State Thruway. I was reluctant to speak, knowing my mindset was more towards the overall well-being of the students who would be placed in the program. My educational philosophy about disadvantaged youth was molded by my days at Berkshire Farm. I sensed the others in the car would not share my sentiments.

Administrator One: "Well, Gregg…I think you know we have you in mind to help lay the groundwork for a program like this at Columbia. What was your takeaway from our visit? You had a long chat with one of the students."

"Yeah. I talked with Donny." I was determined to respond honestly. "Our conversation was insightful but my takeaway is different from yours. I could never be part of a program like the one we visited. Those kids became forgotten students. Like Donny said, '*outta sight outta mind*.' It's a great program to replicate if our goal is to discard and isolate Columbia's at-risk students. But I don't think a program like that is going to help improve the students we're thinking about."

Approaching the Ravena exit on the thruway I wondered…if we truly do not help our at-risk students, could prison for some of them be their post-secondary school reality?

CHAPTER THIRTY-SEVEN

Working Towards an Alternative Program

Do all the good you can,
by all the means you can,
in all the places you can,
at all the times you can,
to all the people you can,
as long as ever you can.

— John Wesley —

The East Greenbush Central School District had several challenging budget years in the late 1990s. To consider implementing an alternative program during fiscally stretched school years was not a popular budget consideration for teachers, administrators, and support staff. Fend for yourself and guard your position for employment survival. The prevailing thought was that if the district was to add a program, then parts of other departments would be eliminated. And as the go-to teacher targeted to lead the program for at-risk students, I was in an awkward position during my early years at Columbia High School.

The Board of Education approved the alternative program advising administration to start on a small scale at the beginning of the next school year. I was asked to teach English 9 and 10 to a group of disconnected students who were primarily discipline problems.

"The classes will be smaller, Gregg." The principal announced at a meeting over the summer. "But you will be dealing with some of our most difficult students."

"How do you decide which students are assigned to those classes?" I asked knowing that any program created simply to be a dumping ground for *bad students* was doomed to fail. "Is there a referral process? I don't think the decision to put a student in the program should be made by one administrator, or a teacher who is sick of dealing with a student in class. I think, without a process, there will be constant complaints and questions why a certain student got in but another one did not."

"I guess we didn't think that far ahead," the principal realized. "We're just trying to get something off the ground. But that's a valid consideration."

"I think that would end up being an issue. How many students are you thinking for each class?"

"Maybe fifteen freshmen and fifteen sophomores," answered the assistant superintendent for instruction. "I think a class that size, even with only at-risk students, could be managed. Do you agree? Fifteen is a significantly smaller class size well below the East Greenbush teacher's contract."

"I think that's a workable number." I paused jotting thoughts and questions in a wire rim notebook. I was determined not to teach an *outta sight outta mind class.* "Maybe we could poll the faculty for a list of students who they think should be admitted, I am sure we would get the names of dozens of students - which is another reason we need a referral process."

The principal nodded in agreement, then asked, "Who would review the referrals and make the determination who is admitted?"

I knew my answer. In my head I have been creating the alternative program for Columbia since our trip to Greene County. "The

Child Study Team meets weekly. That team can review referrals and make recommendations to decide which students would benefit most from being in the program."

"Let's do that." The principal quickly agreed, always looking to avoid predicaments with staff. "Besides, then no one can complain about me not adhering to shared decision making. The Child Study team meets during our Staff Development Days at the end of August before school starts. The referral process will be our first agenda item. But I do need to let the committee know you are willing to take on these two classes?"

"As long as I'm not part of some dumping ground, I'm in."

CHAPTER THIRTY-EIGHT

Building a Program for At-risk Students

You may be disappointed if you fail, but
you are doomed if you don't even try

— Beverly Sills —

Columbia's alternative program began with two English classes. At the end of the year I made a proposal to add another class to the program.

The staff members who helped implement the program met again and there was agreement to expand our efforts with our at-risk population. The principal took off his sport coat and loosened his tie. He sat at a large conference table in a room connected to his office. Handing us a stat sheet about the students in my classes he noted, "Gregg's students are passing his classes and there has been a reduction in discipline referrals and suspensions for those kids. So we want to build on those facts and see if we can increase our class offerings to those students. If we can put together something that is economically feasible for the school budget, I think we will have support from the Board of Education."

"One more thing," added assistant principal Bob as he reviewed the statistics, "the students in the program are staying in school and graduating."

I deflected, "Their academic success is not about my teaching methods." I wanted the team to understand my approach with my students. "The students benefit because I am aware of their challenges both inside and outside of school. And I know the emotional baggage they bring with them to school."

Ted, the other assistant principal and former Notre Dame football player, suggested, "And your kids should get help with their baggage from their counselors and that cost is already part of the guidance department's budget."

"That may be a stretch, Ted," I noted. Counseling for my students was a sore spot for me. "We do need to improve the support services in the program." I quickly remembered that a few guidance counselors were present at the meeting. I was in an awkward situation. I was a member of the same union as the guidance department and we supposedly existed with an unwritten rule never to speak badly about a union member to administration. But fuck it! I was here for my students. "I know there is a counselor listed on their schedules. But most of my students have not seen their counselor since the start of the year. And that was just to get their schedules."

A counselor glared at me, "I doubt that's true, Gregg. And you have to realize that your students are not the only ones on a counselor's roster." Defensively she added, "And your students are not the only students in the building with problems. Our counselors average three hundred students on their rosters."

The principal countered, "But the counselors still have a responsibility to work with Gregg's at-risk students regardless of the size of their rosters."

I don't like being glared at. Union member or not. Some of the guidance counselors shortchanged my students. Flashing back again to Donny's *outta sight outta mind* observation, I responded aggressively, "Listen, I know the numbers are out of whack in your department. Three hundred per counselor is crazy. But maybe a triage approach would better serve the students with the most needs. There is a student in my tenth grade class who is five months pregnant. She told me the whole school knows. She feels ostracized and is very self conscious. But her counselor has not seen her since winter break. She doesn't think her counselor even knows she is pregnant."

Ted chewed on his tooth pick angrily, "That's not a good situation. I'm going to look into that."

"That would help," I responded appreciatively. "The other problem is those kids already feel a disconnect and mistrust with guidance. They would see right through a counselor suddenly showing up and trying to be involved. It will take time and consistent effort to rebuild that connection. We'll have to work through that."

"One way or another," the principal asserted authoritatively, "that issue will be corrected. But today we are here about the budget. Is there anything we can propose to enhance Columbia's alternative program, keeping in mind we're in difficult fiscal times and any proposal will be scrutinized from a cost/benefit perspective."

Bob asked me, "How can we build on what Columbia has in place especially *if* you are still committed to working with these kids?" He looked at me seeking an answer that guaranteed my presence in the program.

"My commitment remains. I have no desire to transfer to mainstream classes. My students already have a history of adults walking out on their lives and I wouldn't do that to them. I won't quit on them." I was sincere in my promise. But I did lose a comrade at the meeting. I noticed one guidance counselor quickly became disinterested as her guilt dripped onto the papers in her binder. Oh dear...

"Let's wrap this up," the principal encouraged, adjusting his black framed glasses. "The board meeting is tonight. Our budget is first on the agenda. And I know that if any board member is against funding additional monies for our at-risk students the argument will be mandatory vs. non-mandatory classes. And the contention will be that we shouldn't be funding a non-mandatory program when state mandated programs also want extra monies. Our presentation must focus on positive outcomes for both students, the building environment, and even the community. And we also need to show that the program is cost effective."

I responded, "I am aware of the tight budget." I reached over and helped myself to a mint from the candy tray. "And I know the union is reluctant about adding classes for the at-risk kids if that is going to impact the job status of members. But we should have faculty support at the board meeting."

"Any suggestions, Gregg?" asked Ted tossing his toothpick into the basket. He seemed distracted by the student commotion in front of the building.

"I think about this a lot. Especially after our union meetings. Everyone is on edge about the budget this year. I worry this may not be the time we should add if we would be taking away. But I also believe my students deserve more in the program. I guess any proposal should be aligned with the goals of the school board. So we should talk about the students passing their classes." I rolled the candy wrapper into a ball. "Maybe distribute these statistics to board members." I held up the document presented to us. "And we should emphasize the reduction in discipline referrals and suspensions, and improved numbers of at-risk students graduating. And hope the board will buy into that success and fund our proposal without cutting from other departments."

"Let's do that," the principal added and suggested that the high school administrators speak about the improvement in discipline. "And Gregg - you can talk about academic achievements and how you work with helping your students improve their lives outside of school. And I will have other staff members there to speak on behalf of the program. Anything else?"

"I also think we should emphasize that the students in the program are not as likely to drop out. And that we work with different human service agencies in the community to help them with other problems. We can present that as a cost/benefit perspective."

The principal was writing away on his legal pad while the assistant principals communicated with each other by eye contact and facial expressions. I could tell they were contemplating leaving the meeting to address the commotion in front of the school.

"Gregg, is there anything specific we can propose for the budget hearing tonight?"

"I think any success with at-risk students is about *contact time.* The more positive contact time the students have with adults in the program, the more likely they will feel connected with the school." I tried to toss my candy wrapper into the basket just like Ted. I missed it. The assistant principal smiled at me. "I was thinking maybe we could add a Life Skills class that I could teach."

Ted, who seemed more concerned with the student chaos in front of the building, turned out to be paying very close attention to the conversation at the meeting. "Look," he said standing from his chair to leave, "I have to deal with the trouble outside but if we want this to fly, Gregg needs to be at the board meeting. He can best articulate the needs of these kids and how much the program is helping them. I think if Gregg is there, we will be adding his Life Skills class to the program."

CHAPTER THIRTY-NINE

CAP — Columbia's Alternate Program

Life isn't about finding yourself.
Life is about creating yourself.

— George Bernard Shaw —

Witnessing the academic gains in my students, along with their increased sense of self-worth and improved attendance, I submitted annual proposals during each school budget cycle in an effort to further strengthen the program by increasing staff, class offerings, and support services for Columbia's at-risk students.

I was determined to secure whatever funding was necessary to best serve the academic and socio-emotional needs of my students. The Life Skills class was added. And throughout the next decade, Columbia's alternative program evolved incrementally.

In the next school budget, two Social Studies classes were added and two more English classes were approved. I was now a full time English teacher in the Alternative Program. And the following year, the junior and senior levels of Social Studies were implemented.

At the annual review sessions with the board of education, I continued to passionately and proudly emphasize how our program benefited the students. The school board then approved the addition of the state required classes for Math and Science. And the next year, a part-time guidance counselor was added to work with our students. I didn't stop there.

My final request was also approved by the school board. The alternative program now employed a full time program assistant to provide academic support, and to be the immediate contact person for families and to monitor student attendance. After seven years of incremental enhancements that seemed like a slow crawl at times, Columbia High School's alternative education program was now complete.

By 2000, I began using the acronym CAP for Columbia's Alternative Program. I referred to CAP in all my interactions with staff, at faculty and board meetings, with my students and their families, and with the human service agencies involved with my students. We were accepted and recognized as a success in the school community. College education departments visited our program. And other school districts sent representatives with the intention of replicating what Columbia offered to their at-risk students.

CAP operated in two classrooms in the North Tower, with an adjacent office on the 3rd floor for our program assistant and for crisis intervention. Our students were with the CAP staff without leaving our floor except for their lab requirements, phys ed, and any electives they needed to graduate. We were engaged with our students for at least eighty percent of their school day solidifying my belief that contact time was essential to academic, social, and emotional growth of at-risk students.

During my final decade at Columbia High School, the school district hired a new principal, John Sawchuk. He was enthusiastically supportive of CAP initiatives. I suggested we increase contact time between our staff and students by assigning our CAP teachers an Academic Intervention period instead of a mainstream study hall assignment. My position was that our staff would get to *know* our students better with the extra contact time. John agreed.

I also asked the county juvenile probation officers, and any other human service agencies working with our students, to have their meetings in our office. They agreed. CAP became a school family for our students; a home away from home.

The final adjustment to CAP was initiated by John. I was surprised. He was younger than our previous administrators and seemed grounded in a philosophy of equity for all students. John understood what CAP was all about. He got it.

"Gregg, I worked something out," John announced walking into my Life Skills class. Our classroom door was closed but that didn't matter to John. The class was discussing abuse in teenage relationships. "You got a minute?"

"Sure. Something on your mind?" I asked with a slight hint of annoyance. My students always thought if a principal came into my class, one of them was in trouble. "I'll give them something else to work on." I redirected the attention of my students away from the distraction of the boss man entering our room.

I was standing over Jen's desk, "Listen...we could go on forever talking about this topic, right? But the discussion is being carried by only half the class. I know each one of you has an opinion about this issue. Maybe even a personal experience. Or you witnessed a friend in an abusive relationship. So your journal this week should be on this topic. And I want you to reference the articles we read and the movie we watched on a teenage abusive relationship, *No One Would Tell.* You learned the red flags. You know the personality traits of most abusers. I want you to write about the manipulation, the control, the vulnerability, and the triggers that are part of an abusive relationship. And to end your journal, in your closing paragraph, discuss where help is available. You learned about those agencies in class. Journals are due on Friday. Write quietly and respectfully. You can get started now. Remember your journals are *always* confidential."

John was already sitting in my teacher chair at my desk. "Make yourself comfortable, John, " I smirked, sliding an absent student's desk over to my teacher desk. "So what's up?"

"I like this class." He offered as an aside. "Your kids like Life Skills, don't they?" He didn't wait for an answer. "Listen...I just got back from a meeting at the Superintendent's Office. Central Administration is on board with your latest proposals to improve CAP. But I've been thinking I should make another proposal."

"An elective for CAP?" I was very protective of the program and didn't want any restructuring without being involved in the decision.

"Not an elective. An addition."

"What are you thinking, John?"

"Yesterday I met with the department chairs. A couple of disagreements. Nothing new. Not my favorite group. I don't see eye to eye with a few of them. And when the meeting ended, I thought to myself, 'why isn't Gregg here?' I mean you created CAP. Built this program up from day one. And you're the *unofficial* leader of CAP. And you also do as much, if not more, than the department chairs. So I think it's time you are recognized as the official leader of CAP."

"I don't look at it like that, John. I don't compare myself to the department chairs. They're about academics."

"OK. You don't see yourself like a department chair. But you know they get release time to oversee their departments and they get extra money for being the chair." John punched my shoulder playfully in a congratulatory manner. "This morning, I got approval for you to be department chair for CAP. You'll get .2 release time, plus a stipend. And if you don't like the department chair title, call yourself the Program Director. But you're now the equivalent of a department chairperson up here."

"Really?" I was truly surprised. "Are you kidding me, John?"

"Nope. Happened just an hour ago at Central and I came right up here. The only downside for you is that you'll have to go to the department chair meetings with me."

****

I remember speaking at a conference on at-risk youth in Savannah, Georgia. My theme was that there are definite predictors to label a student at-risk, but that you never know *when* a student could suddenly become at-risk. I used teenage pregnancies, family breakups, and substance abuse for examples. I emphasized to the group at my session, "you have to *know* your students".

With the building principal's advocacy and a supportive school board, Columbia had a successful alternative program structured in a cost/benefit manner. In presentations I promoted CAP with a *bang for your buck* assessment:

Columbia's alternative program assists up to forty likely to drop out at-risk students for the equivalent of only three full time teachers and one full time teacher assistant.

The final organizational structure for CAP:

- one full time English teacher/Program Director
- one full time Social Studies teacher
- .4 Math teacher
- .4 Science teacher
- .2 Guidance counselor
- one full time program assistant

Take that to the school budget bank.

CHAPTER FORTY

High School Tragedies in Suburbia

There's a lullaby for suffering
And a paradox to blame

— Leonard Cohen —

I always thought of high school as being a sanctuary; a safe haven where teenagers could transcend their problems and find positivity in their lives. But over the course of my career I learned that thought was more a dream than a reality. Many of my most troubling memories from Columbia High School were not related to my CAP students.

I learned an important lesson quickly when I started teaching at Columbia High. My involvement with suburban at-risk students, as an English teacher and Program Director for CAP, did not mean I had a monopoly on *all* the troubled students in the building. There were many other socially and emotionally disadvantaged students in the school and I often wondered how their needs were being addressed. This fact is evident in memories I can't shake of students *not* in the alternate program.

In one single devastating year during the eighties, there were three suicides by Columbia High School students. I was naive. I thought desperately troubled teens were at places like Berkshire Farm and not in a beautiful suburban school in East Greenbush, New York. I was rattled by the tragedies. Although I was a new teacher at Columbia and knew only a small percentage of the student population,

I felt compelled to write an open letter to the student body before the school year ended. I wrote the piece for the student newspaper, *The Devil's Advocate*:

Student suicides - in retrospect

A Columbia High School teacher cites his concern for students

This has been an unfortunate school year; one filled with tragedy and confusion. The shock of our three suicides alone will surely overshadow any accomplishments or pleasant memories we should allow ourselves to cherish.

Pain is such a dominating emotion. But it has always been that way. We allow it to be so. We take our smiles and moments of happiness for granted and then shrug them off. And we permit moments of pain and despair to overwhelm us not realizing the suffering will lessen with time. The result of this thought process is that our smiles become meaningless and those moments of despair are allowed the potential to destroy.

When I heard of Gregory's death, I became disoriented by shock. What the hell kind of world do we live in? Don't people care? I drove into the city where I grew up. I walked the streets I walked as a teenager. The neighborhood hadn't changed much. The city park where I spent so many hours of my youth was still there. The basketball hoops were still without nets. My high school had become a senior citizen home.

It was going to rain. The sky darkened and cracked with warnings of a storm. The scene seemed so appropriate. But who cares? I was feeling bitter and sorry for myself that I existed in such a cold world. When the rain broke through the clouds, I ducked into a shoe repair shop. The owner remembered me. He hadn't seen me in fifteen years. He pointed to the wall near his display of shoe polishes. He still speaks little English. On the wall was a poem I had written as a teenager. It was my first published poem and I gave him a copy. He kept the page from the magazine all these years. He cared.

I walked back into the storm feeling stronger - feeling that if people remember you, they also must care about you. I stopped into Knapp's, the bar whose softball team I used to play on. The same old men sat on the same old bar stools like permanent fixtures watching the ball game. In front of them were shots of whiskey and cheap draft beer chasers.

But they remembered me. "Hey, Kid", they called out in unison. That is the nickname they used to call me, "Kid." I even had that name put on the back of my softball jersey. I was surprised they recognized me. It's been more than a decade since I was in that bar. But they remembered. I guess people do care. All types of people.

****

And that's why I'm writing this. In addition to our smiles and our accomplishments, I think we take for granted just how many people do care about us. Then, when we are feeling down, we think we're alone and that we've been left stranded because we have isolated ourselves from all the people who care.

Life is too damn hard to go it alone. People care. And you are not alone. Remember that. Your only responsibility in a moment of crisis is to let someone know you're feeling down.

If you can't verbalize your hurt, then shed a tear. A single teardrop has an incredibly powerful magnetic effect.

These are tough times to live. I'm sure you feel that way. Teenagers struggle daily to find their identity in a confusing world. Even my nine year old son already fears a nuclear war. That bothers me. A few days ago he wanted to discuss the nuclear themed lyrics of, "It takes a second to say goodbye", by one of our favorite musical groups, U2. Nine years old and he is concerned about a nuclear war. Sometimes I wish he could just play his Little League games and laugh his way through his precious youth.

Tough times. But we can be there for each other and pull each other through. And that's what counts - knowing there are people who will help pull you through.

So I am writing this letter to let you know that I share your feelings. Sure, at times, life can seem unbearable. Sometimes nothing makes any sense. But these moments of pain and despair will pass. Clench your fist. Grit your teeth. Be tough and stay strong. And you can push these moments of pain aside. And much faster even, if you let people who care about you know you are suffering. But you have to let them know. That's what friends are for. Give them a chance. Don't shrug them off. Too many people care. There is no reason for you to lie to yourself and say you're alone and that nobody cares. People do care.

****

I better end here. I could go on forever. Listen. Enjoy your summer. Relax. Have a good time. And do me a favor - OK? Over the summer, think of all the times you smile and laugh.

> Take note of all the times you are around friends and family. And don't isolate yourself. People care about you. Don't ignore these gifts of life. What you're going to find is that you are smiling more than you're sad. And that you're with people who care more than you are alone. You'll feel good once you realize that. You will feel stronger too.
>
> One more thing. If you do happen to find yourself alone, dealing with some troubling incident, and you need someone to talk it over with, call me. My number is 766-2267. I care about you. If I'm not home, call one of your friends or someone in your family. But remember, there are people there who care about you. I mean that. Please remember. So have a good summer. Enjoy yourself. I'll be thinking about you.
>
> (Editor's note: Mr. Weinlein, a Nassau resident, is a teacher at Columbia High School and has written his letter in response to the recent suicides at the school and their aftermath.)

In 2001, another frightening incident occurred at Columbia High School. A student managed to walk up the steps from the lower student parking lot carrying a gun into the school. A massive tragedy was prevented by the heroic efforts of a school assistant principal and a special education teacher. The armed student was tackled and the gun was taken away. Sadly, the teacher was shot in the leg but the tragedy was limited to that injury. Yet the emotional damage was extensive.

That incident forever changed school safety procedures at Columbia High School and at all the other schools in the Capital District. Although only my teacher friend was wounded, the sense of security and safety, and my belief that schools were a sanctuary, were permanently erased from my mindset.

I remember that day vividly. A teacher ran through the halls screaming, "This is not a drill! Armed intruder in the building! This is not a drill!" I followed the post Columbine protocols. The door was locked and my students stacked tables on top of each other. We pushed them against the door and huddled on the floor in the back of the room.

We sat for hours. We received no information over the PA. But we were able to follow live news coverage on the classroom television. A well known local psychologist was being interviewed on the broadcast. He spoke of "The horrific stress and fear the students must be feeling".

During the TV interview a wiseass student asked, "Mr. Weinlein, I missed my lunch period, can we order a pizza?" The tough guy above-it-all attitude of that student quickly disappeared as each classroom was escorted by a police officer down two flights of stairs and out of the building. We walked down the steps single file between a heavily armed gauntlet of SWAT team members.

Reality finally set in for all my students. This was serious. And scary. And so very sad. And our school would never be the same.

CHAPTER FORTY-ONE

A Change in the English Regents Exam

I'm just sitting here watching
The wheels go 'round and 'round

— John Lennon —

"Why do we have to take this test, Mr. Weinlein?" Julie complained as we worked our way through our final review for the New York State English Regents exam.

And Tony chimed in, "Yeah. All my friends like us are taking the school exam. That's the easier test to pass."

"You're answering your own question. We had this discussion before, Tony. I want you to be better than the *easier* way out. And I want you to prove to yourself you are better than the *easier* way out."

On exam day I asked my students to arrive at their regular school time - 7am. The exam started at 8:15. A perfect amount of time for a final review on literary terms. My students were already well versed in their understanding of literary terms, but I felt a final refresher would enhance their confidence.

My teacher's strategy was not to have my students merely be able to define a literary term, but to also have an example. So we listened *again to* the Waterboys', "The Return of Jimi Hendrix" and studied the lyrics. My CAP students willingly engaged in this assignment and had no problem reviewing literary terms by listening to a song about Jimi Hendrix.

I hit the pause button on the player often and asked my students to identify different literary terms utilized by Mike Scott which he sang in a voice blessed with the emotional cadence and heartfelt rhythm of a poet. By the end of the school year, my students had not only mastered the definition of significant literary terms, but they were also able to cite relevant examples.

And much credit goes to Mike Scott's poetic lyrics:

allusion - "He played an encore at the Bitter End..."

imagery - "Scarved, bejeweled, long legged, snake limbed"

alliteration - "Looters sprung from prisons"

internal rhyme - "And straight away began to pray"

simile - "He played my guitar like a lightning storm like twirlin' feathers in the wind"

hyperbole - "His stratocaster caused the mighty Empire State to vibrate"

My students were also confident writers. Not from the formal essays written in class, but from their journal writing. Their weekly journal assignment was structured much like a formal essay. I wanted the CAP students to be comfortable writing a lengthy essay similar to what was required as an appropriate response to a Regents question. The class didn't realize each week they were actually practicing an essay format that would enable them to pass the ELA regents:

Weekly Journal Assignment

Paragraph one - interpret the quote on the board and relate the quote to some aspect of your life or to a piece of literature we read in class.

Paragraph two - summarize the opinion piece from the article and discuss the two positions published in the paper. Conclude the paragraph by stating your position on the topic.

(I utilized the USA Today opinion page which featured a pro/con piece on a current topic. Perfect for my students to become confident with argumentative writing.)

Paragraph three - discuss theme and literary terms utilized in the work of literature read this week.

Paragraph four - Let It Loose! Write about anything on your mind: movies, concerts, favorite songs or television shows, jobs, what's going on at school or at home, relationships, or plans for the weekend.

By the end of the school year my students felt confident in their ability to write a long formal essay. Why shouldn't they? My students were writing more than the equivalent of a Regents essay in their weekly journals.

After our final review I sent my class to the auditorium for the exam. Ten minutes later my students were marching back up the stairs to my classroom.

"What happened? The exam is in the auditorium. Didn't you go there?"

Sean was the first to my doorway, "Mr. Gordon asked us who our teacher was. I told him Mr. Weinlein. And then he said, 'You're CAP students. You should be taking the school exam. It's easier.' And he sent us back here."

"That's not how it's going down, Sean." I was furious. "We're going right back down to the auditorium."

I led my students through the long hallway to the auditorium. Jim Gordon was checking students into the exam. He looked at me inquisitively as I walked up to him. He was the head of the English department. Maybe he was protecting his pass/fail statistics and didn't want to take a chance with my students. "Morning, Gregg. I told your students they should take the school exam in the afternoon. I figured you would want them to do that. Right? It's the easier test?"

"I know, Jim." I was doing my best to restrain myself from blasting him for stereotyping my students. "But I don't want my students taking the easier way out for their English final. We prepared for the exam. They're ready and I want them to take the Regents."

The head of the English department sighed and frowned with disappointment as he wrote down the names of each of my students as they entered the testing area.

A footnote: I taught for another ten years after the new English Regents exam was introduced. In those ten years, ***not one*** *of my students failed the exam. And that statistic includes Brandon, who took his test in the Rensselaer County Jail after he was busted for drug possession, and Marci, who passed the exam while in a drug rehab. Having every one of my students pass that state exam for each of the last ten years of my career, remains my proudest academic achievement.*

CHAPTER FORTY-TWO

Run, Tommy! Run!

I don't even know what I'm hoping to find
Running into the sun, but I'm running behind

Tommy entered the alternative education program after his appearance in family court. The judge, who happened to be a friend of mine, told his parents he wanted Tommy in CAP.

Only a few of my students signed on to participate in extracurricular activities. Most of my students felt a disconnect to Columbia High School. But Tommy was the exception. He signed up for track and announced to his classmates that he joined the team because he runs the "fastest 40 in the damn school." We never had the chance to validate his self-evaluation.

Tommy's reputation for being fast came from his timed runs in gym class and his achievements at elementary and middle school field day events. He was also very successful running from the assistant principals when they raided the woods behind the school to catch student smokers. Unfortunately, our speed demon was not as uncatchable outside of school. Tommy was arrested for "borrowing" things that didn't belong to him and that is why he appeared before my friend in family court.

The practices after school resulted in a very sleepy eyed student who coped by power napping in the CAP office during his lunch period. Tommy never skipped track practice. The slacking off occurred in the classroom. But I learned years ago that working with at-risk teens always involves trade-offs to enable positive involvement in school or in the community.

Tommy's peers patiently endured listening to his daily complaints about the "miles" he had to run at practice just to be on the track team. "I gotta run that shit and Coach knows I can whip any *forty* ass competition at the meets."

"Looking good, T." A few girls said in unison, complimenting Tommy as he entered the classroom wearing his official Columbia High School track attire. He was not a tall student but he quickly grew in stature wearing his Blue Devils tracksuit.

"Look at you, Tommy." I observed standing from my desk. "You even have that *too cool for you guys* look now that you're running track."

"You can't just run good, Mr. W." Tommy pulled a CHS ball cap from his pocket and put it on his head. Backwards of course. "You gotta look good too." He wore gold Adidas running shoes. (Not sure how Tommy afforded those "kicks" and no one ever asked.) His overconfident smile was like a shooting star making its way through a classroom window.

We had a send off party for Tommy on his first Suburban Council Track Meet. This was a big day for CAP. One of our students was running on the varsity team. Tommy was not only representing Columbia High School, but also CAP.

The room was decorated with our blue and white school colors. Streamers and balloons hung from the ceiling. The white board was filled with encouraging messages from Tommy's classmates. And Sabrina and Kaitlyn baked a cake decorated with the words, "Run, Tommy! Run!"

The lights were off in the classroom when our CAP forty-yard sprinter entered the room and was greeted with a rambunctious outpouring from our students, "Surprise, Tommy!"

Unfortunately, Tommy didn't last long running for Columbia High School. After his first Suburban Council Tournament at another school, his promising career as a track star came to an abrupt end. Coach Widner called the CAP office the next morning and said, "We have to meet ASAP."

Outside of school, Coach Widner was a funny and easy going man. But at school his sense of student discipline and student accountability was strict and unwavering. "Did Tommy tell you about yesterday?" The coach asked as we sat at a small table in the CAP office.

"He only told me he didn't run his best race." I looked at Tommy slouched arrogantly in his chair. I sensed the meeting was going to deteriorate quickly.

"His run was fine. I mean...we accept he isn't the most disciplined athlete. He ran mid-pack which is kind of what we expected. Tommy's run wasn't the problem."

The coach wore a white dress shirt and a blue tie around an unbuttoned collar. He was one of a group of veteran teachers, myself included, who thought dress down Fridays were taken to an extreme by the younger teachers who wore concert t-shirts, sandals, and jeans to school. So on dress down Fridays, seven veteran teachers soon to retire, wore dress shirts and ties.

"Tell Mr. Weinlein what happened after the track meet, Tommy. Because when the coach from another school calls me at home in the evening to complain about you...I don't think you're running for the Blue Devils anymore."

Pushing back from the table, Tommy put his hands behind his head. "I don't want to talk about it. It ain't no big deal."

"What did he do, Coach?" I asked, thinking back to our CAP send off party for Tommy and the pride we all felt having a CAP student run varsity track.

Coach was shaking his head, still angry about the phone call. Folding his arms on the table and sternly leaning forward, he revealed Tommy's violation of the athletic code of conduct. "After the track meet we boarded the bus back to Columbia. Tommy was the last to get to the bus. You know...he had to have his time to trash-talk the students from the other school." He flicked his wrist towards the soon to be former member of the track team. "Why don't you take responsibility and finish the story, Tommy?"

Tommy smirked. "That's OK, Coach. You can tell the story better than me." The guilty tone in Tommy's voice reminded me of Lennie in *Of Mice and Men, 'I done another bad thing.'*

I sensed my CAP junior was uncomfortable and nervous. I wanted to move the meeting along before Tommy did or said something to get himself into more trouble. "I'm anxious to hear what happened, Coach. Can you just tell me?"

"Yeah. But I'm not surprised he doesn't want to talk." The coach's facial expression was flushed with disgust. "Tommy, when you do something wrong, take ownership. You screwed up. Big time. Like I said Mr. Weinlein, the team was already on the bus. All our runners, our team manager, the assistant coaches, trainers. And I'm standing at the door waiting for your CAP student. Then I hear the home school coach screaming to Tommy, 'Hey, get back here! Get back here with that!' And Tommy walks towards me, like he has no sense of right and wrong, carrying *their* starter block." Coach Widner was looking for an admission of guilt, "Right, Tommy?"

Tommy answered with a shrug of his shoulders.

Coach Widner continued to depict what he was told in the phone conversation with the other coach. "Their coach said he was screaming and running after Tommy. He said he was pissed and still yelling, 'You damn punk. Hey, I'm talking to you! Don't you dare get on that bus with our starter block!'"

"And your CAP student walks up to me, as nonchalant as can be, while I'm checking off names for the bus back to Columbia, and I said, 'Tommy, what the hell are you doing with their starter block!?' I was furious. Embarrassed, I said, 'Tommy, we're the visiting team. We don't have a starter block here.' Their coach was still screaming, 'Get your butt back here with that!'"

"But Tommy wasn't concerned at all. He didn't care. I got in Tommy's face and yelled, 'Do you hear me, Tommy? *We don't have a starter block here!* We're the visiting school. We **DON'T** have a starter block here.' And Tommy just smiled. He looked at me and said, 'You do now, Coach.'"

CHAPTER FORTY-THREE

A Former CAP Student Is Published in Her College Literary Journal

I'll stand my ground
won't be turned around...
and I won't back down

— Tom Petty —

A few years after I retired, a large envelope arrived in my mailbox from the English Department of a local college. I was not expecting the package. I stood in the driveway and opened the envelope. A Post-it note was placed on the cover of the school's literary journal:

"Mr. Weinlein - I wrote this thinking about you. Thanks again for all your help - Sarah."

Thanks, Mr. Weinlein

Sarah Pfeiffer

This year marks ten years that I have been tromping through life unabashedly stating, "If it wasn't for Mr. Weinlein, I wouldn't have graduated high school". I realize this sounds a little extreme, but by the end of my freshman year, I was fast approaching the family tradition of not graduating.

After a childhood of going through the motions with my mouth shut and my eyes down, I found myself suddenly, and uncontrollably, angry. I skipped classes, hung out with the wrong people, and spent my time getting to know the staff in the principal's office. As you can imagine, the avalanche of so-called 'help' ensued: reprimands followed by several meetings with my mom, ended up with detention, suspension, and counseling. Of course, that simply cemented the idea that I was a bad student who didn't care.

In reality, I was a teenager, struggling through adolescence, and finally reacting to all the compartmentalized memories and emotions of a highly dysfunctional childhood. Add to that the confusion of being a gay youth in the late nineties, and you've got yourself a kid who can't be helped. That is, until I was introduced to Gregg Weinlein.

In a last ditch effort, I was set up to meet with the director of my school's alternate program. Sitting at the first meeting, slumped, inwardly rolling my eyes, I listened to Mr. Weinlein explain why the alternate program was different. The class sizes were much smaller, the students had classes with only a few teachers who taught multiple subjects, and everyone was there to support each other no matter what. The last part got my attention. 'You mean, if I have a problem I can go to you and talk about it even if I have to miss a class?' Without hesitation, Mr. Weinlein answered, 'Anytime. My door is always open.' I felt sure this was some sort of trap, and made it my personal mission to expose this clearly fake support.

I was now in classes of ten or twelve peers, rather than the standard twenty or thirty. I experienced teachers who looked you in the eye, and didn't let you get away with anything less than your best, even if your best wasn't good yet. I found myself amidst passionate debates that sometimes exploded in the middle of a lecture, and were encouraged to continue. Over time, the feeling amongst the students was that of acceptance, camaraderie, and pride to be part of something bigger than themselves. Through it all, I watched a single man shoulder the weight of several titles: administrator, teacher, counselor, father figure, and friend. That same man faced opposition, anger, and politics from every angle with a kind heart and a strong conviction. Without knowing it, he taught us to do the same.

Today, I sit surrounded by my college textbooks, and think of how far I've come in my life. I have a beautiful wife, and incredible people filling all areas of my world. I have owned a stain glass business, owned a house, and traveled to Europe. I have experienced extraordinary things, beautiful moments in time that make me ask myself: would this all be possible if I hadn't graduated high school? The answer that I found is this: I have the courage and conviction to get to where I'm going no matter what, but it sure doesn't hurt to have a leg up along the way. Thanks, Mr. Weinlein.

CHAPTER FORTY-FOUR

A Change in Dropout Perspective

When you're standing at the crossroads
And don't know which path to choose…
I'll stand by you

— Chrissie Hynde —

In the decade before my retirement, CAP became a well-regarded program by teachers, administrators, the board of education, and other schools in the Capital Region. Although most educators and stakeholders viewed CAP as a successful dropout prevention program, I always felt Columbia's Alternate Program had a more wide ranging impact on the lives of our students than simply holding onto them until they had a diploma.

I noticed early on in my career at Columbia High School that students who dropped out often gravitated to playing the victim by blaming the school and avoiding any sense of individual accountability for their educational setbacks:

- "...the school didn't want me there"
- "...Columbia did nothing for me"
- "...they don't care"
- "...teachers don't even give you a chance to pass"

Not once did I hear, "I'm dropping out. I'm failing everything because I never did the work." Or, "I probably shouldn't have missed sixty days of school." Don't misunderstand, I am not saying school does not play a role in the reason a student drops out. But the proliferation of alternative education programs in our public schools shows that the proverbial light at the end of the tunnel was finally turned on and schools realized they need to help and support *all* students.

Even in the early years of CAP when the program consisted of only a few classes, there was limited student engagement. Having students in our classes for only a small fraction of their school day did not allow for the needed contact time to bring about change. As a result, the school blame game remained the standard excuse if one of our students dropped out. But with the added classes, and a mass effort to change perceptions that our program was just for "bad kids," CAP became a viable and positive educational alternative for students with at-risk challenges.

I remember a meeting in the CAP office with Paulie. His mother requested the meeting to formally withdraw her son from school. She sat nervously in an office chair. Subdued, as she held Paulie's two year old sister. Our social worker, Mrs. Benoit was also present.

"Are you sure about this, Paulie?" I asked as the social worker handed me the withdrawal papers already signed by my student's mother.

"I just can't do it anymore, Mr. W."

"But you're passing all your subjects?" I wanted Paulie to reconsider. "You're even passing Phys Ed - which you failed every previous year in high school until you came into CAP."

"I know. But I'm always just catching up and like I never seem to really get there." A look of somber reality engulfed his face. "Even the gym class. I got to take gym class every day of the week. Some days twice with my schedule. I know it's because I failed all the other years before CAP but I just don't want to do this anymore. I fucked up for too long in school."

"We don't talk like that here, Paulie," the teacher in me said.

"And I don't want you talking like that anytime around your mom. Be respectful."

Mrs. Benoit joined the conversation. "I've been on the phone several times this week with Paulie's mother. And they are set on their decision, Mr. Weinlein."

"Paulie, you know I want you to change your mind, right?" I looked at both Paulie and his mother hoping for an outcome that I knew was unlikely. "Your attendance has been so good this year. Did you ever see your attendance record before you came into CAP?" I was desperate and threw out every positive educational spin I could invoke. "You were missing so much school before CAP, but now you're coming to school."

Paulie's mother offered an insightful observation. "I think that's part of the problem, Mr. Weinlein. He's only been in CAP for four months...and he has been going to school like you said. But before CAP, school was like an every other day thing. I'd get him to come here one day and then he would refuse to go the next day. Or he'd take a few days off. And that never seemed to be a problem for the school." Paulie's sister interrupted, dropping her pacifier onto the floor. I bent down and retrieved the binky. Mom added, "Before CAP I was always threatening him about Columbia's attendance policy. You know...the Code of Conduct you have. But Paulie knew if he refused to go to school, all that would've happened was detention or he would get suspended and fail anyway. He figured, why bother? He had years of not going to school regularly and to start going now is like too much for Paulie."

"Is your PO on board with you quitting, Paulie?"

"I'm sixteen." Paulie answered. "She said I have to get a job if I drop out or she's gonna violate me."

"Probation isn't going to do anything if Paulie doesn't go to school." The mother's frustration was obvious. "He doesn't get into trouble. He just doesn't go to school. And Paulie's like an adult now. I can't force him. And I have my baby to take care of."

"Well...you know I'm against you dropping out. I wish there was more we could do to keep you in school, Paulie." I surrendered.

"It's time to move on, Mr. W," Paulie said. "You guys did what you could. I chose not to come to school all those years before CAP. You're always saying in Life Skills class to take responsibility. To take ownership for decisions you make. I never liked my teachers before CAP. I never did school work before CAP. I know I'm a senior but I gotta quit. I'm dropping out, Mr. W. But at least I learned to believe in myself from your program."

Paulie's mother validated her son's comment. "That's true, Mr. Weinlein. For the first time since grade school, Paulie was in a program that worked for him and I wasn't getting phone calls every day from teachers and principals to complain about my son. Before he got into CAP all I ever got from school were complaints. Never anything positive. Besides, it's not like Paulie's going to college or anything. His uncle owns a tree service and Paulie has worked with him on weekends since he was twelve years old."

I stood up accepting that my student was withdrawing from school. I opened the top drawer to the metal file cabinet in our office to get one of our newly designed long sleeve CAP shirts. We rewarded our students with a shirt for good attendance, academic achievement, or acts of kindness and courage. On the upper left front was the school image of a Blue Devil. Below the Blue Devil was printed, *CAP - Columbia's Alternate Program.* On the back was printed a Bob Marley lyric, "*Who the CAP fits / Let them wear it.*" I handed the shirt to Paulie, shook his hand, and said, "Whenever you wear your CAP shirt, I want you to think of us."

"I get this?" Paulie asked, surprised. "I thought you had to do something good to get one. And I'm not. I'm dropping out."

“But you did, Paulie. You did something real good when you finally said you believe in yourself.”

“Thanks, Mr. W. And I won’t forget you guys.” He lifted the baby from his mother’s arms and helped her from the chair. Together they walked out of the CAP office for the final time.

Paulie dropped out. But we were beginning to solidify an important change in perspective and attitude about our students who quit school. Paulie took responsibility for his educational situation. He didn’t need to blame the school.

Months later, the buzz in CAP was about a sold out metal concert at the Upstate Music Hall by the band, Gwar. Several of our students had tickets to attend. The next morning, Dina charged into our attendance period towards my desk. “Mr. Weinlein! Guess who I saw last night?” She didn’t wait for my guess. “I got a picture on my phone.” I expected to see a close up photo of the band. “Look,” she said with excitement, putting her phone close to my face. “It’s Paulie! And check out the shirt he’s wearing. See? He wore it to the Gwar concert!”

And on Dina’s screen was a smiling photo of Paulie wearing his CAP shirt.

CHAPTER FORTY-FIVE

Hiring a CAP Teacher

These are better days…
There's better days shining through

— Bruce Springsteen —

My perspective on education differed immensely from my colleagues. Mine was shaped by a career working with at-risk, socially disadvantaged students, and by my own treacherous climb out of adolescence. I taught believing a student's life and my ability to know, support, inspire, and redirect was more important than the English lessons in my classroom.

During interviews with candidates applying for positions in CAP, I was often responded to with a confused, uncertain look as I articulated my educational philosophy. I needed to know that the candidate hired would be competent teaching a class composed of only at-risk students. As each candidate spoke of their teaching abilities and highlighted achievements in their resume, I inserted my educational philosophy. I informed the applicants that working in CAP was not like teaching mainstream classes. "You have to remember that on any given day *academics may have to become secondary to your lesson.* On those days, your lesson plan takes a back seat to what is going on in their lives."

I have a fond memory of one interview. The interview team consisted of the department leader, myself, and a representative from administration. Four applicants were scheduled. Each one had an outstanding resume to show as they discussed their academic successes and classroom methodologies. Two candidates taught in the honors program at their school. Another candidate was teaching at a junior college. But the last interviewee spoke of the sensitivity and respect needed to be successful teaching socially disadvantaged students. She had experience working with at-risk teens.

Connie said her students needed "another way." She talked of helping her students improve their lives through self-respect and education. At mid-interview I found myself bored. I no longer wanted to listen. Four candidates and three hours in a cramped department office. I was tired. I already knew Connie would be the best fit for CAP. Let's end the chatter and perfunctory questions. No need to continue going through the motions. I know...not very professional, right?

I guess I began to fade out as others on the team continued with the interview. I know I zoned out. Connie told me so when I saw her a few months into the school year at McGeary's Irish pub in downtown Albany.

"Hey, Gregg...?," she asked, holding a sixteen ounce plastic cup of Coors Light as she moved towards me away from her group of friends. Black 47, an Irish rock band from NYC, played under a tent outside the pub. "I've been wanting to ask you something about my interview." She took a long gulp of beer. "And I guess I've had enough to drink to come right out and ask you."

I was sipping a Guinness and enjoying the Indian summer evening as the band blasted through a string of rebel songs. Connie had transitioned smoothly into her teaching position in CAP. She was respected and she *knew* her students. And she was solid with her academic demands in the classroom. So what about the interview?

"Was there a problem? You sailed through the questions and made a great impression on everyone."

"You." Connie answered. "You were the problem."

"Me?" Chris Bryne was rapping the lyrics to his brilliant song, *It's time to go.* On weekends I religiously gravitated to a noneducational mindset. If I went out for a couple of pints and to hear music, I wanted to avoid talking shop. But I knew from the intensity of Connie's brown eyes staring at me that she was adamant about questioning me. This seemed personal. And more than a query regarding the framework of the interview. "Did I say something wrong? I had you pegged right away to be the CAP teacher."

"Well...you didn't come across that way." Her head bobbed to the beat of *Funky Ceila.* "Do you remember how you acted? When the interview started you were taking the lead with your questions. You asked about what I knew about the challenges teaching at-risk students. And you asked about my willingness, my confidence, and strategies I would use to get to know and connect with the students in your program. All questions which I anticipated when I was preparing for the interview."

I wasn't sure where this was going. "And they were the same questions I asked the other candidates." My Guinness went down smoothly.

"I'm sure. But I was certain by your body language that my responses didn't match up with what you were looking for. At one point, I thought you even smirked." Connie lit a cigarette, which surprised me because I didn't know she smoked. But I guess the raucous pub setting was appropriate for a smoke.

"I'm not sure I'm following you, Connie. Seems crazy you think that. I liked your responses to everyone's questions. I thought you hit a homerun."

"Then why weren't you engaged for the rest of the interview? I sat there thinking *if this guy is the program director, he's not hiring me.* You made me so nervous. I felt defeated. I was certain I wasn't getting the job."

"You're kidding? That was not it at all."

"Then what was it, Gregg? Why did you act that way? I wish the interview was taped so I could show you. You looked so bored and like you didn't want to be there."

I smiled. I got it. I remembered the interview vividly. Connie was right. I *was* put off by the mundane predictable questions that continued to flow. Afterall, I already got the responses I was looking for. "I need another pint. Let's get another beer?"

We stood together in line at the portable bar waiting to be served. "I'm sorry I made you feel that way, Connie. I probably suck at the whole interview thing. And I guess I did cash out after you answered my questions. But *not* because I didn't think you were the best candidate for the job." I ordered another Coors Light and a Guinness. I touched Connie's shoulder gently. "And I should know that disengagement and acting bored is not appropriate for an interview." *Now* I was smirking. "And definitely should not be part of a formal professional interview to hire a teacher." I handed Connie her beer. "I would have hired you just talking to you here at McGeary's. I just felt I had a good read about you."

"Really, Gregg...I don't give a crap about what you think of interviews. I felt like shit when I left. I really wanted the job and you acted like I didn't stand a chance."

"Sorry." I took a long sip of my freshly poured Guinness. "I guess I thought to myself *let's stop wasting time and just hire Connie.*"

Connie shook her head in disbelief. "You're different." She tapped her plastic pint against mine. "Let me put it this way, Gregg - you really know how to make a first impression on teachers coming into CAP."

CHAPTER FORTY-SIX

Teacher Awards

I learned more from a three minute record
than I ever did in school

— Bruce Springsteen —

Fortunately, my interview techniques were not prerequisites for three teacher awards. The Teacher of Merit Award was presented to me by Senator Joseph Bruno at a ceremony in Troy, New York. I was also honored as an Outstanding Teacher by a local television station. The other award was from the New York State English Council. I enjoyed the benefits of the awards, especially from News 10 who videotaped a conversation with me and interviews with my students.

I waited until the morning of the visit to tell my students.

"I have an announcement. We're going to have visitors during Period 5 today."

"More Siena College students?" Sherry asked, looking annoyed,

The visits were initiated by a retired superintendent of the East Greenbush School District who was now an adjunct professor at Siena College. I welcomed the visits. Too many higher education programs did not offer experiences to familiarize future teachers with socially disadvantaged students. I was more than willing to give the Siena students opportunities to observe our program. I also thought about the positive reports that the students would bring to their college for their class presentations.

"Who keeps sending them here?" Mariah griped. "It's like every week."

"I hope Siena keeps coming here," Tony hoped. "Some of them girls are *hot*."

"Sorry, Tony. The visitors this afternoon are from News 10. Elaine Houston, the evening news anchor, will be visiting to learn about CAP. And she will bring along a cameraman from the station."

"I know her! I see her on TV." Jamie stood to check herself out with a pocket mirror she stored in her bag. "Why they doing that, Mr. W? Why are they coming today? Crap. Look what I'm wearing!" She gestured with her hands rejecting her school uniform of baggy sweatpants and a too large music t-shirt. "If you gave me a heads-up, I wouldn't wear this."

"Don't worry, Jamie," Tony commented. "Mr. W. ain't gonna let you nowhere near the camera dude. You'd ruin the video."

Alexis asked, "Why are they coming to CAP?"

The classroom door opened abruptly. Principal Sawchuk barged in. He moved quickly to the center of the room in front of the class. "Did you tell them, Mr. Weinlein? Your students know about today? Do they know why?"

"I was just beginning to tell them."

"I'll finish letting them know." He turned to the class. The sleeves of his dress shirt were rolled up for proper muscle notice. Muscle exposure was part of his administrative attire. "You kids should be proud today." He took note of one of my students. "Sit down, Jamie."

Descending into her seat, a very annoyed Jamie asked, "Why you storming in here to Mr. W's class? Why you telling me to sit down?" Jamie continued to stand defiantly. "You ain't our teacher." Jamie, like most students in CAP, had very little appreciation for public school hierarchy.

"If you can check your attitude for a minute, I'll tell you why."

The principal waited for Jamie to sit down. "Mr. Weinlein won the News 10 Teacher Award. Not a mainstream English teacher like you'd think. Not a Science teacher. Not a Math teacher. *Your* CAP teacher. I'm sure Mr. Weinlein feels honored. But I want you to be proud of your teacher...and of yourself. It's because of your progress in the program that Columbia was able to provide documentation showing why Mr. Weinlein deserves the award. So I just wanted to tell you...and keep up the good work. And make sure you are on your best behavior when the television crew arrives."

Mr. Sawchuk entered the classroom with noticeable flair. But he exited quietly in a very slow strut often mimicked by my students.

"Jesus, Mr. W - that's awesome. How much money will you get?" Brendon asked as he high-fived his classmates sitting around him.

"This isn't about cash, Brendon. I'm guessing I will get some type of certificate." My response stifled Brendon's enthusiasm. "Why? Did you expect a cut if there was prize money?"

Jamie interjected, "But it's still cool that Channel 10 is coming here to see us," She was so stressed about her on-camera appearance.

"Super cool," added Tyler from the back row.

"Well I know someone's gonna get something from your award, Mr. W." Jamie noted with a piercing sardonic tone.

"Who's that, Jamie?" Tony asked.

"For damn sure, Sawchuk will be in here to get his picture taken."

The CAP segment on News 10 was repeated throughout the week. Watching the news each morning as I dressed for school, I felt validated that CAP was indeed recognized as a significant educational program. Soon after the segment aired, I received requests from several teachers and administrators from other schools to observe our program and to discuss how their school could replicate CAP.

****

The Teacher of the Year honor by the New York State English Council included a trip to NYC for their annual conference where I would receive the award. I was surprised by this award. Granted, my *notch in my belt* memory of teaching English in CAP was that not one student of mine ever failed the Regents exam. Still, I never considered myself an "academic" teacher - the type who is usually the recipient of these awards.

Mr. Sawchuk was notified about the award. I'm sure he was also behind this nomination. But I didn't expect the conversation that ensued when I was paged to his office.

"You hit the jackpot again, Gregg. Great news for you and for CAP."

"No kidding, John. I was really surprised. My only connection with the English Council was a poem I published in their journal back when I was teaching at Berkshire Farm."

"Well…it should be a great time for us." (Here we go again. Principal Sawchuk was working his way into the awards banquet. And Jamie was not here to set things straight!)

"What do you mean?"

"NYC. The Marriott Marquis. We bring the wives. Treat them to a nice dinner and a night on the town. And we will have it all paid for through the district's conference fund."

I stood quietly in front of the principal's desk. He handed me the conference request form his secretary had already completed. I glanced at the document, noting the two dates for NYC and the two rooms requested for the Mariott Marquis. When I looked at the date I realized I had a problem with an overnight stay in the city. "I'll bring it up to my wife tonight and let you know tomorrow."

"Sure. But you have to go." The principal spoke with authority. "You should be excited. I even put in for train fare. Neither of us have to drive and we can just relax on the ride down to Penn Station. Let me know tomorrow. But this is quite an honor, Gregg. And the district will love the recognition and the pictures we bring back from the ceremony. Talk to the wife...and see me in the morning so we can firm things up."

I was appreciative of the award. But I shied away from formal social events. I'm not sure why. I always avoided holiday parties, happy hours with the Columbia staff, group conferences, and even retirement parties. I even requested my Social Studies teacher, a good friend of mine, put a stop to his organization of my own retirement party.

My school social activity was limited to our six am teacher basketball games every workday morning. Even after a knee surgery, I still went to the gym and watched until I was cleared to play again. Those games were the extent of my social scene at Columbia.

The thought of a couples trip to NYC with the principal and his wife had no appeal to me. And the date was a major issue for me.

"Good news and bad news, John." I informed the principal the next morning in his office. "The good news is I'm up for the awards ceremony in the city."

"Of course you are." John anticipated, turning from the large window where he watched the students getting off their school buses. "Bad news?" He walked behind his desk and leaned forward pushing his arms onto the glass desktop. "What's the bad news? The trip is all set up for a nice getaway for you and the wife."

"The kids are still young, John. We really don't do overnights, and we're not comfortable leaving them that long with a sitter for a day trip to the city. We appreciate you setting everything up, but we just can't stay overnight. My wife won't go. She insists on staying home. But I'm still game for taking the train down with you."

"But what about you? I'll get you a room at the Marriott."

I took a deep breath. I knew my answer would not be welcomed. "Can't, John. I would feel like crap leaving my wife home for two days alone with the kids. They're really young. We just haven't done that stuff. I checked the agenda and I can go. But I'm getting the five o'clock train back after the awards are given out."

Slumping into his large black leather chair, the principal unveiled a look of pressure and disbelief. "You can't stay overnight? Everything's paid for."

I was beginning to feel uncomfortable. My reason was something of a white lie as I refrained from admitting the truth about why I was not staying overnight. "Just wouldn't feel right, John. But I'll be with you and your wife for the train down and we can hang together during the day. Have a few drinks. You know?"

Leaning back into his chair, John cupped his hands together under his chin. "Jesus, Gregg." His head swayed from left to right. "This is a mess now."

"What do you mean? You guys still get away from here. No school. And you have two days in the city. Your wife will have a great time."

"Yeah. Right." John dropped his hands from his chin and placed them onto his thighs as he pushed himself up from his chair. "My wife and I are going because of your award but you're not even staying overnight. How's that look for me - if I stay overnight and I'm not at school the next day and you're at school."

I not only anticipated John's reaction, but also his question. "John, the event goes into the evening. With dinner and speakers, and the social gathering after, I don't think you'd make the last train to Albany on a weeknight and I'm thinking my principal is telling me to take tomorrow off." My principal seemed very appreciative of the suggestion.

I didn't see John and his wife all day once we left Penn Station. At the conference I visited a few exhibits and attended a seminar. I skipped the gathering for the conference lunch and opted for a cup of soup and a few pints of Guinness at McHale's Pub, a few blocks north of the hotel.

At the awards ceremony I sat with John and his wife in the back of the large ballroom. "Did you sit in on anything today, John?" I didn't wait for an answer. I knew John wouldn't attend any of the events. I poured coffee from the carafe and made small talk with John's wife. "This must be so boring for you?"

"Not really," she answered. "After we checked in we did some shopping on Fifth Avenue so I'm having a great time. What about you, Gregg?"

"I checked out a few things after we got here. But I wish I had slept on the train. I'm tired already. I made my way to a favorite Irish pub in the city for lunch. I think I spent more time sipping Guinness than I did at any seminar." John and his wife smiled. The ballroom was filled with educators. The scene was chaotic.

"These big conferences never go off as scheduled," John noted with wandering eyes. "It seems so disorganized. The award presentations were supposed to start twenty minutes ago."

I shuffled through my papers in the NYS English Conference folder. As an aside, and trying to keep a positive vibe knowing I wouldn't be staying much longer, I commented, "You guys look great." John wore a royal blue suit with a silk tie and looked professionally dapper. His wife looked stunning. "I've never seen you dressed up like this before."

"All for the CAP English Teacher of the Year," John smiled.

I watched the ballroom clock tick away. As the hours passed, and the awards ceremony still had not begun, I knew I had to depart to catch the 4:45 Amtrak home.

I excused myself from the table and walked up to the woman who appeared to be the conference organizer. I stood next to her while she finished her conversation with another attendee wearing the same NYSEC name tag I wore. And then she turned to me.

"Hi." She looked at my name tag. "You need help with something, Gregg?"

"Not really. I just wanted to let you know I have to get a train back soon. I have an evening commitment in Albany and I won't be able to stay for the awards ceremony. But my principal is staying." I pointed to John. "Could you give my certificate to him?"

"Oh, Lord...I'm so sorry. I know we're running late. You really can't stay? It's such an honor to be an award recipient?"

"I'm very honored." (I think I was sounding quite professionally honored, just like I was supposed to be.) "But I do have to catch the late afternoon train back."

"I apologize again, Gregg. This afternoon is playing out like an absurdist drama, Gregg. (Now if we were going to see a Sam Beckett play I would have stayed.) You're the teacher of at-risk students, right?" I nodded. "We were so touched by the package your principal sent to us...staff letters, letters from your parents, and your students. We were so glad to recognize someone who does the work you do. We need more teachers like you in our schools willing to work with these students."

"Thank you," I responded appreciatively. "And I'm sorry I can't stay but I have a very important commitment and I have to leave in a few minutes."

"I understand. The awards segment should have concluded by now. We just can't seem to get our act together. At least let me go and get your award certificate. I'll be right back."

"Thanks. I'll be at our table."

"What's up, Gregg?" John inquired. I didn't even sit back down.

"Remember I told you I couldn't stay overnight and would be leaving early. The organizer said the awards ceremony should have ended by now. She's getting my certificate. Can you bring it to school for me? I have to take off." I tried to lighten the conversation. "So I'll be out of here and you guys get to tear up the city tonight on your own."

"You're not even going up on the stage for your certificate? I thought we could get some photos for the school and your students."

"We can take them right here when she brings back the certificate. I'm sorry. I told the kids I would be home before they go to bed." The guilt of my spin was starting to bother me.

"Family first, Gregg," acknowledged John's wife. (Thank God!) But now the guilt of my white lie was really bothering me. Standing, she took her camera out of her designer bag.

We took our photos with my New York State English Council certificate in hand and then I left. I exited the awards banquet down the steep escalator and hustled myself onto 7th Avenue.

I called my wife as I dodged the madness on the streets of Times Square. "Hi. I got out." I was panting as I dodged the manic traffic at the intersection of 42nd Street and 7th Avenue. "I'll be able to catch the train. Can you be outside the station? Don't forget my change of clothes: sneakers, jeans, and my Yankee hoodie. And can you bring my Stone Pony hat? Thanks. Are you excited? Yeah…me too. It's going to be great. Thanks. Yes. I'll be careful. See you in a few hours."

I ran down 7th Avenue fitting right in with the chaos on the streets. I took off my sport coat and tie faster than Clark Kent as I sprinted towards Penn Plaza. I thought about the awards ceremony and leaving my principal and his wife behind. And I thought about my white lie for the reason I left early and could not stay overnight.

I had to make the Bruce Spirngsteen concert at the Pepsi Arena in Albany.

Yes. I bolted from a formal education event to attend a concert of real life education. Laughing and racing between the hordes of people and impatient traffic, I shouted out the lyrics to my Awards Banquet theme song by The Boss:

"We learned more from a three minute record…than we ever learned in school."

CHAPTER FORTY-SEVEN

My Hamlet — The Death of My Student

One more time to feel the light,
I know you're standing by my side.
Knuckles white, grasping tight on
your memory fading out of sight,
So I, yes I tried,
I put you in a shadow box.

— Molly Durnin —

There is darkness today. Even the angels weep as the piercing, fierce, and soulful licks from Pat's guitar torch the sad midsummer sky.

I was one of Pat Tiernan's teachers. Like most of my students, Pat did not connect with the high school scene. His world was beyond the books, assignments, school dances, sports, and the typical games of teenagers. His world was his guitar. As his teacher, I always felt lucky because I managed to keep Pat in class instead of finding him in the cafeteria playing his guitar.

But Pat was not just one of my students. Pat was also my Hamlet. I called him Hamlet in school. I called him Hamlet at his music gigs after he graduated. And even when we exchanged emails, I referred to Pat as Hamlet.

Years ago I took a musician friend from Australia to Stout, a downtown bar, for Pat's open mic gig. Of course I introduced my friend Travis to Pat and said, "This is my former student. You can just call him Hamlet." Even when anyone told me they were going out to see Pat play, I would tell them to call him Hamlet. And Pat would know who sent them to his show.

How did Pat become my Hamlet? The answer goes back to when Pat was in my English 11 class. The majority of my students had little interest in reading the books which were part of the department's curriculum. Actually, most CAP students didn't even want to be in school. So the thought of teaching Shakespeare to my students was as remote a possibility as asking Pat to cover a Justin Bieber song.

But I knew shortly after Pat entered CAP, that he was a special student with excellent reading skills and an extensive vocabulary. And there was also something special about his voice. Not just the clarity, but also the enthusiasm that graced his tone when he read. There was the gift of song in Pat's voice.

When Pat read aloud, the words boomed rhythmically off the pages of the text. Would I finally attempt Shakespeare now that there was a student with the reading and verbal skills to read a play like *Hamlet*? I was game for trying. I assigned Pat the part of Shakespeare's most troubled prince.

Together, we read every single line in Shakespeare's play aloud. I am certain the class was more attentive because their classmate was an engaged reader of the play. And that is how Pat became my Hamlet. I was so proud my students listened attentively and even seemed interested in my explanations and interpretations of the drama.

For a classroom reward for getting through the play, I organized a field trip to the Palace Theater in Albany for a performance of *Hamlet*. I know, being an English teacher, I am supposed to promote *all art* as wonderful. But this performance was horrendous and I was embarrassed I dragged my students to such a mediocre production.

One evening, years after his graduation, I went to see Pat's band play. During a set break we sat together in a booth and talked about school. I asked if he remembered going to see *Hamlet* at the Palace. I even admitted that I thought the performance sucked. (Funny how honest you can be once someone is no longer your student.) I think I was even apologetic. "At least a lot of the class took off and split to McGeary's parking lot across the street for a smoke."

Pat looked at me with guilt in his eyes and a grin on his face. I never met anyone who could feel remorseful and still flash the brightest of smiles. Pat possessed that rare talent. Even though more than ten years have passed since Pat was my student, he still couldn't call me by my first name. Respectfully Pat confessed, "Mr. Weinlein, I was one of your students who took off for the parking lot for a smoke."

How special was it to have Pat in my classroom to assume the part of Hamlet? Like I said, I never would have attempted Shakespeare with my students unless I had the right student to carry the class through the play. That night in the booth at the bar, I had my own confession. I told Pat I *never* taught Shakespeare again in CAP after he graduated.

At Pat's funeral, I was a sorry sight trying to say good-bye to my Hamlet and to be strong enough to console his former classmates. This good-bye was just too much to bear:

- my student gone so early in life
- my student who was such a talented musician
- my Hamlet - a bluesman with such a happy heart

I was without adequate and comforting words. Standing arm and arm with two of Pat's closest friends near his coffin, I could not even pretend. Finally, to bid farewell, I uttered the words Hamlet spoke upon the death of Horatio. Words Pat would know. Words more appropriate and more beautiful than any words I could put together kneeling at Pat's coffin:

"Good night, sweet prince / And flights of angels sing thee to thy rest."

CHAPTER FORTY-EIGHT

The End of a Career

And sometimes I wonder
Just for a while
Will you ever remember me

— Tim Buckley —

Five veteran teachers met in Gerry's classroom during fifth period lunch. We referred to our sessions as "counseling" periods. In April, four of those teachers handed in their retirement papers. I was the holdout. For the last three months of the school year, I became the focus of our therapy sessions.

"Look…I'll spell it out for you." Jeff began writing numbers and retirement jargon across the blackboard with a broken piece of chalk.

"We're all retiring." Gary added. "Don't you get it? You did your time."

I answered sheepishly. "I do but…"

"Why would you want to spend another year with these maggots?" Steve questioned pacing up and down the aisles between the desks. He was frustrated by my lack of desire to retire considering all the counseling that was coming my way. "You're gonna hang out with your cutesy English teachers for another year?"

"Look at this, Gregg." Jeff demanded, squatting to the floor to pick up broken pieces of chalk. And then as an aside, "Gerry, can't you get a goddamn white board!? Your blackboard has to go." And back at me, "Seriously. Look at the facts. They're right here." He tapped the chalk vigorously against the board. “Your pension may not increase for years if you don’t retire now and don’t take the incentive.”

“He’s right, Gregg.” Gary confirmed, his large body looked silly squeezed into a student chair. “That incentive is our ticket out of this place.”

Steve continued impatiently, “Yeah. That’s right. You could end up working several more years just to get what you’re going to get this year if you retire.”

The group stared at me waiting for a response. “I don’t know.” I tried to explain my uncertainty. “You guys have been telling me this for months now. I hear you. But I just don’t know.”

“Two months! Two damn months we’ve been telling you since we heard the incentive was coming,” Jeff commented, disappointment dictating his tone. “You got thirty-five years in.” He turned towards Gerry. “Tell him. Tell him, Gerry. You’re with him every morning.”

“He knows.” Gerry leaned back in his cushioned teacher chair and put his feet up on a slew of student papers scattered across his desk. “I talked to him again this morning when I drove him to school.”

“Well…what the hell doesn’t he get?” Steve asked. “The shit is black and white. Right there on the board.”

“Same thing. I told him the same thing we’re telling him here. He knows.”

“I do know. I get it.” Gary eyeballed me for confirmation. I felt my uncertainty was letting my counselors down. “And I appreciate you guys explaining all this to me.” I scanned the room nodding my sincere appreciation to my colleagues. “I just never thought of myself as being retired. Never looked at numbers. Didn’t even have a clue about incentives until our therapy sessions.”

“And this session’s about to end in two minutes,” warned Gary, pointing to the clock on the wall.

“Yeah,” Steve foreshadowed. “The maggots will be charging in here." And with sarcasm added, "For another one of Gerry's brilliant lectures." We laughed.

"Gregg, listen to me." Jeff walked from the blackboard to where I was seated. "The numbers tell us it's time to go. Our pension with the incentive is close to our salary. We may never get those numbers again. We're all in the same boat with the monthly amount we'll get. And we don't have a clue when or if another incentive will come down. Don't know what else we can tell you. I don't know. Gerry doesn't know. Steve doesn't. And Gary doesn't know. But why work more years just to get the same amount of money that you would get if you retire now?"

Steve offered a humorous insight, "Gregg thinks he has to work for the rest of his life. That's what you get when you marry a younger woman. You get young kids at home when you're supposed to be thinking of retirement."

"Steve's right," Gary paused at the doorway. "How old are the kids now?"

"Twelve and nine." I answered as I stood and reconnected the clasp of one of the silver ID bracelets I wore on my wrist. The names of my children were engraved on each bracelet. I was relieved this counseling period was about to end.

Cognitive therapy with my three closest teacher colleagues was becoming uncomfortable. Not painful. More like when you are sitting in your therapist's office and you are at a point where you know you have to take action. And it's obvious that it's time you stop listening and time for you to act. You have to do something.

In my head I heard Joe Strummer of the Clash singing, "Should I stay or should I go?"

And then Seanchaí barged into my head singing, "It's time to go."

Gerry walked to the door to greet his students. He made a closing comment to conclude the group counseling session, "Remember what I said in the car this morning, Gregg? Retirement for you will be different. We will all get similar pensions. But you get a bonus. You get to be home with your kids while they're growing up. That should be all the incentive you need."

And that was it.

Not the numbers Jeff outlined on the board. But realization that I had the opportunity to be a stay-at-home Dad, with a teacher pension, while the children were still young.

The next morning, I announced my retirement to Mr. Sawchuk.

Word spread quickly. My legacy was built with the creation of CAP and the fact that for thirty-five years I taught only at-risk students. Many colleagues of mine who began their careers in CAP left as soon as an opening occurred to teach mainstream classes.

But I stayed.

Gregg Weinlein

An at-risk teenager, **Gregg Weinlein** transcended his challenges through education and became an award winning high school English teacher. Throughout his thirty-five year career, Gregg taught socially disadvantaged students. Since his retirement, Gregg has spoken at conferences, published articles on education, consulted on alternative education programs, and facilitated seminars on best practices for working with at-risk students.

Gregg's climb from his adolescent years of drugs, alcohol, and relationship issues is vividly portrayed in his memoir, *Been There / Taught That.*